The Australian Women's Weekly

the great CHICKEN COOKBOOK

Ellen Sinclair
Food Editor

New Dual Measurement Edition

Golden Press
Sydney

Contents

Oven Temperatures

Electric Temperatures

	Fahrenheit	*Celsius*
Very slow	250	120
Slow	300	150
Moderately slow	325-350	160-180
Moderate	375-400	190-200
Moderately hot	425-450	220-230
Hot	475-500	250-260
Very hot	525-550	270-290

Gas Temperatures

	Fahrenheit	*Celsius*
Very slow	250	120
Slow	275-300	140-150
Moderately slow	325	160
Moderate	350	180
Moderately hot	375	190
Hot	400-450	200-230
Very hot	475-500	250-260

Cup Measures

	Metric	*Imperial*
1 cup flour	140 g	4½ oz.
1 cup sugar (crystal or castor)	250 g	8 oz.
1 cup brown sugar, firmly packed	185 g	6 oz.
1 cup icing sugar, sifted	185 g	6 oz.
1 cup shortening (butter, margarine, etc.)	250 g	8 oz.
1 cup honey, golden syrup, treacle	375 g	12 oz.
1 cup fresh breadcrumbs	60 g	2 oz.
1 cup packaged dry breadcrumbs	155 g	5 oz.
1 cup crushed biscuit crumbs	125 g	4 oz.
1 cup rice, uncooked	220 g	7 oz.
1 cup mixed fruit or individual fruit such as sultanas, etc.	185 g	6 oz.
1 cup nuts, chopped	125 g	4 oz.
1 cup coconut, desiccated	90 g	3 oz.

Cup and Spoon Measures

Recipes in this book use this standard metric equipment approved by the Australian Standards Association.

(a) 250 millilitre cup for measuring liquids. A litre jug (capacity 4 cups) also is available.

(b) a graduated set of four cups—measuring 1 cup, half, third and quarter cup—for measuring items such as flour, sugar, etc. When measuring in these fractional cups, level off at the brim.

(c) a graduated set of four spoons: tablespoon (20 millilitre) liquid capacity; teaspoon (5 millilitre); and half and quarter teaspoons.
Note: All spoon measurements are level.

All about Chicken

There's a wonderful variety of recipes in this book from which to choose: a selection of the world's most famous classic ways with chicken; family meals; party dishes; salads; superb pâtés; and specialist recipes from some of Australia's best-known restaurants.

This first section gives basic information on chicken: how to joint, how to bone, basic methods of cooking, plus a selection of stuffings and sauces.

Chicken Sizes

Packaged chickens are available in a number of unit sizes, determined by weight.

For instance, a No. 12 chicken weighs 1.2 kilograms (about 2¼ lb.); a No. 15 chicken weighs 1.5 kilograms (3 lb.), etc.

Chicken pieces are a useful buy; they allow you to choose the cut of chicken best suited for any particular dish. Pieces usually available are breasts and half-breasts, cutlets or thighs, Maryland (combination of thigh and leg), legs, breastwing (combination of breast and wings), wings, chicken breasts, chicken fillets (breasts removed from the bone) and backs (good for soup).

For many recipes—particularly those to be served with a white or cream sauce—some cooks prefer to remove the skin of the chicken before cooking. However, for those recipes where the chicken pieces are browned before cooking, the skin browns more easily and gives protection to the juicy meat beneath.

Basic Methods of Cooking

Roasting

Two methods of roasting are given below. For the usual method of roasting, allow approximately 25 minutes per 500 g (1 lb.) in moderate oven. For the French method of roasting, water or stock is added, and a moderately hot oven is used for cooking.

Roast Chicken

1.5 kg (3 lb.) chicken
prepared stuffing
salt, pepper
60 g (2 oz.) softened butter

Chicken can be roasted with or without a stuffing. Place chicken in baking dish, rub breast and legs well with 60 g (2 oz.) softened butter; sprinkle with salt and pepper.

Roast in moderate oven until tender, approximately 1¼ hours for 1.5 kg (3 lb.) bird; brush bird occasionally with pan juices.

To test if chicken is cooked: the leg will move easily when moved to and fro gently with the fingers; the skin will start to shrink from the bones slightly; when the chicken leg is pierced with a skewer at the second joint, the juices will be clear, not pink.

French Roast Chicken

1.5 kg (3 lb.) chicken giblets
prepared stuffing
60 g (2 oz.) softened butter
1 cup water
1 chicken stock cube
salt, pepper

Chicken can be roasted with or without a stuffing. Place chicken in baking dish, rub breast and legs well with 60 g (2 oz.) softened butter; sprinkle with salt and pepper. Add 1 cup water, 1 crumbled chicken stock cube and any giblets from chicken to baking dish.

Roast in moderately hot oven until tender, allowing approximately 1¼ hours for 1.5 kg (3 lb.) bird; add extra ½ cup water during cooking time if water evaporates too much; baste occasionally with pan juices.

Serves 4.

Boiling

Method 1: Half-fill large saucepan with cold water, add one peeled and roughly chopped onion and carrot, and salt and pepper. Place chicken into water, cover, bring to boil; reduce heat, simmer approximately 45 minutes to 1 hour, or until tender, drain and cool. (Water in which chicken was cooked can be used as basis for soup etc.)

Method 2: Fill a large saucepan with water, cover, bring to boil; place chicken in water, cover immediately, bring water back to boil, turn off heat, leave chicken in water until completely cold, preferably overnight. This is a useful method when chickens need to be cooked in quantity.

Steaming

A whole chicken or chicken pieces can be cooked in a steamer, over boiling water; water should be kept at a rapid boil. The food does not touch the water, but is cooked with the steam. Place a piece of greased greaseproof paper over chicken pieces so that they are protected from condensation dripping from the lid; make sure that the lid of saucepan fits securely, so that steam does not escape. Allow approximately 30 minutes per 500 g (1 lb.) cooking time, but this will vary with thickness of chicken pieces used.

Chicken can also be steamed in a pressure cooker.

Shallow Frying

This is cooking in enough oil (or dripping etc.) to come half-way up side of food; that is, when the food is turned there is sufficient oil to cook and brown the other side. Chicken to be shallow fried does not necessarily require a protective coating; once the juices have been sealed in, by placing chicken into hot oil, heat can be reduced and chicken cooked over medium heat until brown and tender. Chicken can also be dipped in flour or egg-and-breadcrumbed before being shallow fried.

Deep Frying

This is cooking in enough oil (or dripping etc.) to two-thirds fill a deep pan or electric deep fryer. There should be enough oil to completely cover the food, and allow it to circulate around the food. Do not overcrowd the pan. Add food gradually to oil, so that heat is maintained. Lower food gently into pan to prevent splashing.

Deep-fried chicken generally has a coating, such as batter or breadcrumbs. This protective coating prevents the chicken from becoming dry during cooking. Chicken can be boiled or steamed until just tender, cooled, then battered or crumbed, and then deep fried in hot oil until coating is golden brown and chicken is heated through.

Double Frying

If raw chicken is to be deep fried, double frying gives the best results. Crumb or batter chicken, deep fry in oil which has been heated to medium heat only. Cook until chicken is just tender, and coating lightly browned. Remove chicken from oil, drain on absorbent paper. Chicken can be fried again for immediate serving, or cooled and refrigerated several hours, or overnight, and fried again just before serving.

To fry again: reheat oil until hot, lower chicken into pan, fry until golden brown; chicken will be cooked through at this stage.

Grilling

Brush chicken pieces with melted butter, place on greased grill pan, grill under medium heat until browned and tender. Brush chicken several times during grilling with melted butter. When grilling chicken breasts, flatten breasts slightly to allow even browning.

Cooking on a rotisserie

Chicken can be filled with a stuffing, if desired. Tie legs together firmly; tie wings so that they are held firmly against the body. Brush chicken with melted butter or oil, sprinkle with salt and pepper.

Insert the large skewer, or probe of rotisserie, through centre cavity of chicken, secure at either end with the small skewers; tighten screws well so that chicken is held firmly and securely, as chicken shrinks during cooking. Chicken should be evenly balanced so that it will cook correctly. To check balance, place chicken, in rotisserie position, in cold oven, turn roto motor on; if chicken is correctly positioned, skewer will turn evenly, without jerking.

Cooking instructions vary, according to type of rotisserie fitted; follow manufacturer's instructions. As a general guide to cooking time, allow approximately 20 minutes per 500 g (1 lb.) in a moderate oven.

Defrosting Frozen Chicken

1 Thaw chicken at room temperature for at least 12 hours, depending on weather.

2 Take chicken from freezer compartment of refrigerator, place in lowest part of refrigerator to thaw; this will take from 24 to 48 hours.

3 To defrost a chicken quickly, place chicken in a new plastic bag (often plastic bag in which chicken is packed is damaged slightly and water could seep in), secure top tightly. Drop chicken into sink or basin of cold water, leave at least 3 hours, or until thawed. Or put chicken in sink and run cold water over it.

Sauces and Stuffings

A savoury filling adds extra interest to a simple roast chicken, and helps increase the size of each serving. We give recipes here for two stuffings, plus some interesting sauces.

Herb Stuffing

2 cups fresh breadcrumbs
30 g (1 oz.) butter
2 tablespoons chopped parsley
1 teaspoon grated lemon rind
2 teaspoons mixed dried herbs
1 small onion
salt, pepper
1 egg

Sauté chopped onion in butter until transparent. Add onion and the butter to remaining ingredients, except egg; mix in beaten egg to bind.

Pineapple Stuffing

⅔ cup long grain rice
450 g can crushed pineapple
½ teaspoon thyme
1 tablespoon chopped parsley
1 medium onion
1 egg
salt, pepper

Gradually add rice to large quantity of boiling salted water, boil rapidly 10 to 12 minutes or until rice is tender; drain. Drain pineapple.

Combine rice, pineapple, thyme, parsley, peeled and finely chopped onion, egg, salt and pepper; mix well.

Creamy Wine Sauce

60 g (2 oz.) butter
1 medium onion
2 tablespoons flour
⅓ cup dry white wine
1 cup chicken stock
pinch cinnamon
pinch nutmeg
salt, pepper
30 g (1 oz.) butter extra
½ cup cream
½ teaspoon lemon juice

Melt butter in saucepan, add peeled and finely chopped onion, sauté until transparent. Remove from heat, blend in flour; return to heat, stir constantly 2 minutes, remove from heat, gradually stir in combined stock and white wine. Return to heat, stir until sauce boils and thickens.

Reduce heat, simmer 2 minutes, add cinnamon, nutmeg, salt and pepper. Add extra butter gradually, stir until melted. Add cream and lemon juice, reheat gently, without boiling.

Gravy for Roast Chicken

1 tablespoon flour
1 cup water
1 chicken stock cube
salt, pepper

Remove cooked chicken from baking dish. Pour off any surplus fat, leaving about 2 tablespoons in dish. Stir in flour, cook gently until flour mixture is light golden brown.

Remove from heat, add crumbled stock cube, gradually stir in water; return to heat, stir until sauce boils and thickens, reduce heat, simmer 2 to 3 minutes.

Season with salt and pepper.

Giblet Gravy

250 g (8 oz.) giblets
1 cup water
1 small onion
1 stick celery
15 g (½ oz.) butter
3 teaspoons flour
salt, pepper

Combine roughly chopped giblets, onion, and celery with water in saucepan, bring slowly to boil; cover, reduce heat, simmer 15 minutes; strain, reserve liquid.

Melt butter in saucepan, stir in flour, cook 1 minute. Gradually stir in reserved stock, stir over medium heat until gravy boils and thickens.

Season to taste with salt and pepper.

Bread Sauce

1 medium onion
3 whole cloves
½ bayleaf
2 cups milk
1½ cups fresh breadcrumbs
salt, pepper
15 g (½ oz.) butter

Peel onion, stud with cloves, combine in saucepan with bayleaf and milk. Bring slowly to boil, cover, reduce heat, simmer 5 minutes; strain, reserve liquid, discard onion and bayleaf.

Add breadcrumbs to reserved liquid, season to taste, with salt and pepper, simmer gently until mixture is creamy; stir in butter.

how to joint a chicken

Many of the recipes in this book call for chicken pieces to be used; these can be bought in most large food stores or delicatessens. However, if you're only able to buy a whole chicken, and have to joint it yourself, the pictures show you the correct way to do it. You'll need a good sharp knife and a pair of poultry shears or a strong pair of kitchen scissors.

1

Cut through skin connecting leg to body; bend leg out, away from body, find the joint where leg hinges, cut through this (there's no need to cut through bone).

2

Cut each leg into two pieces at joint, as shown; this gives thigh and drumstick. Or the leg can be left in one complete piece.

3

Cut a slice of breast meat with the wing to make a better serving portion, then bend wing away from body to find joint where wing joins body; cut through this.

4

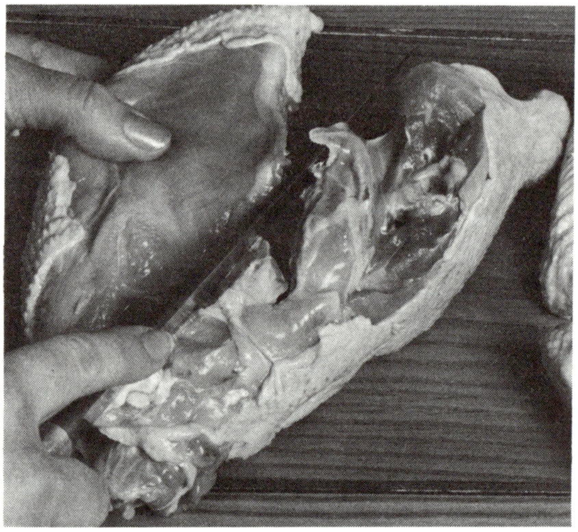

Separate breast and back by cutting through rib-bones along each side of body; cut as close as possible to backbone.

5

Turn breast section over, cut down centre of breastbone to divide breast in two; trim away any excess skin and fat.

6

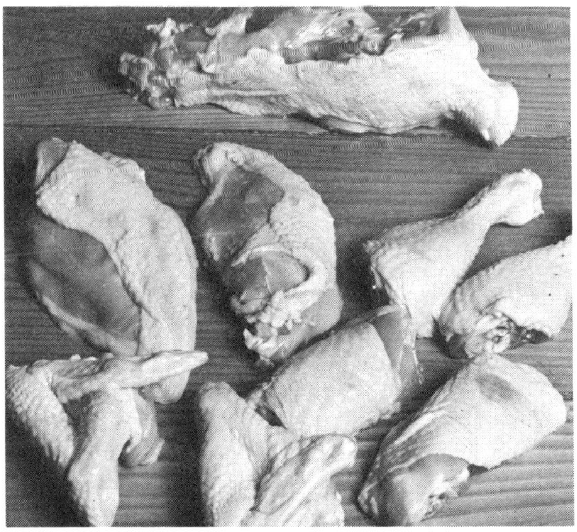

Picture shows the jointed chicken. Back portion is not considered as individual serving portion, but can be served to accompany another portion, such as a wing, or used to make soup etc.

to bone a chicken

A chicken can be boned, and the inside filled with a savoury stuffing · Boning takes a little time and trouble, but is worth the effort.

1

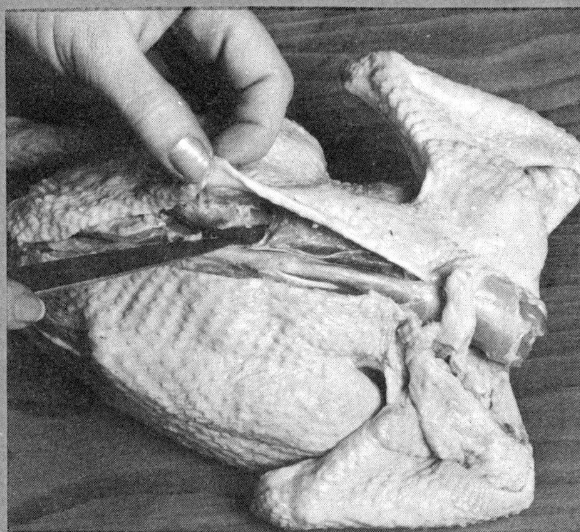

Using a sharp knife, cut through skin of chicken, down centre back. Using tip of knife, separate flesh from back bone on both sides.

2

Following shape of bones of chicken with knife, gradually ease bones—in one piece—from flesh, cut loose with knife as shown. (Bones are left in legs and wings.) Spoon filling into chicken, secure cut piece at back with skewers.

Main Courses

Chicken is one of the most versatile of all foods; it will gain compliments for the hostess when presented in a delicious way at the most important dinner party, and it is equally right for family meals, luncheons, barbecues and holiday picnics.

Almond-Garlic Chicken

2 whole chicken breasts
salt, pepper
90 g (3 oz.) butter
1 small clove garlic
2 teaspoons chopped parsley
3 tablespoons flour
1 egg
125 g (4 oz.) finely chopped blanched almonds
30 g (1 oz.) butter extra

Mushroom Cream Sauce:

3 shallots
2 teaspoons flour
¾ cup cream
190 g can champignons
1 teaspoon lemon juice
salt, pepper

Remove chicken breasts from bones (giving 4 individual pieces), pound each piece with mallet or rolling pin until thin, sprinkle with salt and pepper.

Cream butter, add crushed garlic and chopped parsley, mix well; refrigerate until firm. Place quarter of butter mixture at one end of each chicken piece, fold in sides, roll up, secure with small skewers. Roll in flour seasoned with salt and pepper, dip in beaten egg, then roll in almonds; press almonds on firmly. Refrigerate 30 minutes to firm coating. Place rolls in shallow greased oven proof dish, spoon over extra melted butter, bake uncovered in moderate oven 35 to 40 minutes, or until chicken is cooked through and tender. Drain excess butter from dish, reserve for sauce.

Serve sauce separately.

Mushroom Cream Sauce: Place reserved butter into small pan, add sliced shallots; sauté 2 minutes.

Stir in flour, cook 1 minute; remove pan from heat, stir in cream. Return to heat, stir constantly until sauce boils and thickens.

Reduce heat immediately, add drained champignons, lemon juice, salt and pepper; mix well.

Serves 4.

American Fried Chicken

1.5 kg (3 lb.) chicken pieces
2 cups milk
1 teaspoon salt
¼ teaspoon pepper
¼ teaspoon nutmeg
1 teaspoon dry mustard
½ teaspoon thyme
1 teaspoon paprika
flour
oil for deep frying

Combine milk, salt, pepper, nutmeg, dry mustard, thyme, and paprika in bowl, add chicken pieces, cover, refrigerate several hours or overnight. Drain chicken; reserve the milk.

Coat chicken pieces in flour, dip into the milk, re-coat in flour. Add chicken pieces gradually to hot oil, deep fry approximately 15 to 20 minutes or until chicken is golden brown and cooked through, turning occasionally.

Serve with salad or vegetables.

Serves 4.

Apricot Chicken

1.5 kg (3 lb.) chicken pieces
2 medium onions
60 g (2 oz.) butter
1 tablespoon cornflour
425 ml can apricot nectar
salt, pepper
125 g (4 oz.) dried apricots
½ green pepper
½ cup sour cream
1 tablespoon soy sauce

Heat butter in large pan, brown chicken pieces well on both sides; remove from pan.

Add chopped onions to pan-drippings, sauté a few minutes. Blend cornflour into apricot nectar, add to pan, stir until sauce boils and thickens. Reduce heat, season to taste with salt and pepper, add dried apricots, cut in halves.

Return chicken to pan, simmer, covered, 30 minutes, or until tender, stirring occasionally. Add green pepper, cut into thin strips, cook further 5 minutes. Stir in sour cream and soy sauce, reheat gently.

Serves 4.

Almond-Garlic Chicken—chicken breasts, rolled, coated with finely chopped almonds, then baked until tender. There's a creamy mushroom sauce as accompaniment.

Beggar's Chicken

This is one of the renowned dishes of the Orient, and visitors to Hong Kong or other parts of the East take away with them the memory of this dish—the tenderest, most succulent of all chicken dishes. The legend is that, in ancient China, beggars who stole chickens had to devise some way to hide them while they were being cooked, to escape detection. So they buried the chicken in a hole with sand or soil. The chicken, complete with feathers, was encased in clay and thrown into the hot fire. When cooked, the clay was broken away, taking the feathers with it, leaving behind the steaming brown chicken.

We've devised a thick paste, as a substitute for clay, so that Beggar's Chicken can be cooked at home, in the oven. It cooks to such delicious tenderness, the meat falls from the bones.

1.5 kg (3 lb.) chicken
3 shallots
1 teaspoon sugar
2.5 cm (1 in.) piece green ginger
4 tablespoons soy sauce
1 teaspoon water
flour
water extra
90 g (3 oz.) butter
2 teaspoons brandy
¼ teaspoon ground ginger
¼ teaspoon five-spice powder

Chop shallots; combine with sugar, crushed green ginger, soy sauce, and 1 teaspoon water. Spoon into chicken. (1 cup cooked rice can also be mixed in.) Secure vent with small skewer. Make a paste of about 2 tablespoons of flour and 1 of water. Spread over vent to seal as securely as possible.

Rub chicken well with softened butter, combined with brandy, ginger and five-spice powder; rub in well.

Wrap chicken in well buttered aluminium foil, securing like a parcel so no steam can escape during cooking. (Banana leaves, well-greased, can be used in place of foil; in China, lotus leaves are used.)

Roll out clay-paste to about 1 cm (½ in.) thickness. Place chicken in centre and fold clay around, smoothing to make sure there are no holes through which steam can escape. Try not to have overlapping areas of clay which are too thick to allow the heat through easily.

Place on oven tray. Bake in hot oven 2 hours.

Remove from oven, break clay gently with mallet or hammer, remove from round chicken. Handle carefully—it's really hot!

Lift the foil-wrapped chicken on to plate, peel back foil from top of chicken, or tear it away.

Clay-Paste:

3¾ cups cooking salt
3 cups plain flour
1½ cups water, approx.

Clay-Paste: Place unsifted flour and salt into basin, mix with sufficient water to make a firm dough. Knead until smooth on lightly floured board.

Serves 4.

Brandied Chicken

1.5 kg (3 lb.) chicken pieces
2 large onions
90 g (3 oz.) butter
1 tablespoon oil
1 teaspoon curry powder
salt, pepper
½ cup cream
1 tablespoon brandy

Peel and slice onions. Heat oil and butter in saucepan, add onions, sauté until transparent; add curry powder, sauté 2 minutes.

Add chicken pieces, cover, simmer over low heat 30 minutes, or until chicken is tender. Season with salt and pepper, add cream and brandy, reheat gently.

Serves 4.

Chicken a la King

1.5 kg (3 lb.) chicken (or chicken pieces)
1 small green pepper
30 g (1 oz.) butter
125 g (4 oz.) mushrooms
2 teaspoons grated onion
1 tablespoon flour
salt
1 cup cream
3 egg-yolks
2 teaspoons lemon juice
½ teaspoon paprika
2 tablespoons dry sherry

Steam or boil chicken until tender; drain, reserve ½ pint of the chicken stock. Remove chicken meat from bones, cut into large dice.

Remove pith and seeds from green pepper, chop finely, cook in boiling water 5 minutes, drain.

Melt butter in saucepan, add green pepper, sliced mushrooms, and grated onion; sauté a few minutes. Remove from heat, stir in flour and salt, return to heat, cook, stirring 2 minutes. Gradually stir in cream and stock; add chicken. Stir until sauce boils and thickens, reduce heat, simmer 3 minutes.

Stir a little of sauce into beaten egg-yolks, return to saucepan. Add lemon juice and paprika. Reheat gently, stirring; do not boil. Just before serving, stir in sherry. Serve with hot rice.

Serves 4.

Chicken Alexandra

1.5 kg (3 lb.) chicken (or chicken pieces)
90 g (3 oz.) butter
4 medium onions
½ cup boiling water
1 bayleaf
salt, pepper
1 cup cream
300 g can asparagus cuts

Cut chicken into serving-sized pieces, sauté in 60 g (2 oz.) butter until just changing colour. Melt remaining butter in separate pan, add finely chopped onions, cover, cook until soft. Add boiling water and bayleaf, cover tightly, simmer gently 30 minutes or until water is almost absorbed. Remove bayleaf.

Put in blender with cream, blend on high-speed 1 minute, or push through sieve.

Return to saucepan, add chicken pieces, cover, simmer gently until tender. Stir in asparagus with liquid from can, leaving a few asparagus pieces for garnish, heat gently. Season to taste with salt and pepper.

Serves 4.

Chicken and Almonds

4 whole chicken breasts
1 teaspoon salt
1 tablespoon cornflour
1 egg-white
1½ tablespoons dry sherry
oil for deep frying
125 g (4 oz.) green beans
2 sticks celery
½ red pepper
125 g (4oz.) mushrooms
½ 230 g can water chestnuts
2 tablespoons chopped shallots
30 g (1 oz.) toasted almonds
2 tablespoons oil extra

Sauce:

1 cup water
1 tablespoon soy sauce
1 tablespoon cornflour
1 chicken stock cube

Bone chicken breasts, cut meat into 2.5 cm (1 in.) pieces or strips, combine with salt, cornflour, lightly beaten egg-white and sherry in basin; mix well. Deep-fry chicken pieces in hot oil until just changing colour; drain.

String beans.

Cut beans, celery and pepper into 2.5 cm (1 in.) strips, slice mushrooms. Drain water chestnuts, cut in half. Heat extra oil in large heavy-based frying pan, add vegetables, sauté until just tender, add chicken, heat thoroughly. Place chicken mixture on to serving dish, top with sauce, sprinkle with toasted almonds.

Sauce: Blend cornflour with soy sauce and water, add crumbled stock cube. Stir constantly over heat until sauce boils and thickens.

Serves 4.

Chicken and Asparagus Casserole

1.5 kg (3 lb.) chicken (or chicken pieces)
2 tablespoons flour
salt, pepper
2 tablespoons oil
250 g (8 oz.) small white onions
1 small green pepper
470 g can asparagus cuts
440 g can cream of mushroom soup
1 cup water
½ teaspoon mixed herbs
1 bayleaf

Joint chicken, coat lightly with flour seasoned with salt and pepper. Heat oil in large frying pan, add chicken pieces, cook until golden brown.

Remove from pan, place chicken in large greased ovenproof dish.

Peel onions; add to pan with green pepper cut into large dice, cook 5 minutes. Put on top of chicken, add drained asparagus cuts. Combine soup, water, herbs, bayleaf, salt and pepper, pour over chicken and vegetables.

Cover, bake in moderate oven 1½ hours or until chicken is tender.

Serve with rice.

Serves 4.

Sweet-and-Sour Chicken

2 kg (4 lb.) chicken pieces
2 tablespoons soy sauce
1 tablespoon sugar
½ teaspoon salt
1 tablespoon dry sherry
1 egg-yolk
2 tablespoons oil
2 onions
8 shallots
125 g (4 oz.) mushrooms
1 red pepper
1 medium cucumber
450 g can pineapple pieces
oil for shallow frying
1 tablespoon cornflour
¼ cup vinegar
1 tablespoon tomato sauce
salt, pepper

Bone chicken pieces, cut into 4 cm (1½ in.) cubes. Combine soy sauce, sugar, salt, sherry, and egg-yolk in large bowl, add chicken, marinate 1 hour. Heat oil in large saucepan, add sliced onions, cook until transparent. Add chopped shallots, sliced pepper, and mushrooms; cook further 5 minutes. Add cucumber cut into chunky strips, and drained pineapple pieces (reserve syrup); cook few minutes; remove from heat.

Drain chicken from marinade, reserve liquid.

Heat oil for shallow frying, cook chicken pieces until golden brown; drain well. Add chicken to vegetables. Blend cornflour with reserved pineapple syrup; add vinegar and tomato sauce, stir into reserved marinade. Bring to boil, stirring constantly; season to taste. Pour sauce over chicken and vegetables, stir to coat evenly. Reheat gently.

Serve with hot rice.

Serves 4 to 6.

Chicken Bercy

1.5 kg (3 lb.) chicken (or chicken pieces)
125 g (4 oz.) butter
125 g (4 oz.) small mushrooms
2 shallots
¼ cup dry white wine
¾ cup water
1 chicken stock cube
3 tablespoons tomato sauce
salt, pepper
1 tablespoon flour
chopped parsley

Cut chicken into serving-sized pieces, sauté in hot butter until brown, remove from pan.

Add sliced mushrooms and chopped shallots to pan, sauté a few minutes. Stir in flour, cook 1 minute. Remove from heat, gradually add wine and water, blend well. Return to heat, stir until sauce boils and thickens. Add crumbled stock cube and tomato sauce; season to taste with salt and pepper.

Reduce heat, return chicken to pan, simmer, covered, until tender.

Serve sprinkled with chopped parsley.

Serves 4.

Chicken Bordelaise

1.5 kg (3 lb.) chicken (or chicken pieces)
4 onions
185 g (6 oz.) mushrooms
155 g (5 oz.) butter
1 cup dry white wine
1 cup water
2 chicken stock cubes
salt, pepper
1 tablespoon tomato paste
¼ cup flour
1 cup water extra
400 g can artichoke hearts
chopped parsley

Chop two of the onions finely, slice mushrooms. Melt 30 g (1 oz.) butter in saucepan, sauté onions and mushrooms until lightly browned. Add wine, water, and crumbled stock cubes, simmer until reduced to half quantity. Stir in tomato paste, season to taste with salt and pepper.

Cut chicken into serving-sized pieces. Melt 90 g (3 oz.) butter in separate pan, sauté chicken until brown on all sides, remove from pan.

Add flour to pan, cook 1 minute. Remove from heat, gradually add extra water. Add the mushroom sauce, return to heat, stir until sauce boils and thickens. Return chicken to pan, simmer, covered, until tender.

Cut remaining onions into thin slices,sauté in separate pan with artichoke hearts in remaining butter 5 minutes. Sprinkle chicken with chopped parsley, garnish with onion rings and artichoke hearts.

Serves 4.

Chicken Croquettes

1¼ cups milk
4 peppercorns
1 onion
1 carrot
45 g (1½ oz.) butter
⅓ cup flour
500 g (1 lb.) cooked chicken
250 g (8 oz.) mushrooms
60 g (2 oz.) butter extra
2 egg-yolks
salt, pepper
1 egg
packaged dry breadcrumbs
oil for deep frying

Combine milk, peppercorns, sliced onion and sliced carrot in saucepan. Bring to boil, reduce heat, simmer 5 minutes; strain; reserve milk, discard vegetables.

Melt butter in saucepan, remove from heat, stir in flour, return to heat, cook, stirring 1 minute. Gradually stir in reserved hot milk. Stir constantly over heat until mixture boils and thickens.

Sauté finely chopped mushrooms in extra butter until just tender; drain. Chop chicken finely.

Add mushrooms, chicken, egg-yolks, and salt and pepper to sauce, mix thoroughly. Spread mixture evenly on greased tray which has been covered with greased greaseproof paper. Refrigerate until cold and set. Divide mixture evenly into 16 portions. Mould each portion into croquette shape about 6 cm (2½ in.) long. Dip in beaten egg, press breadcrumbs on firmly.

Refrigerate 1 hour.

Deep-fry in hot oil until golden brown.

Makes 16 croquettes.

Chicken Divan

1.5 kg (3 lb.) chicken
750 g (1½ lb.) fresh broccoli or 2 x 375 g packets quick-frozen broccoli
boiling salted water
90 g (3 oz.) butter
⅓ cup flour
½ cup cream
2 tablespoons dry sherry
salt, pepper
2 tablespoons grated parmesan cheese
extra parmesan cheese

Steam or boil chicken until tender, drain, reserve 2 cups of cooking liquid. Remove bones from chicken, cut meat into serving-sized pieces, keep hot.

Discard large part of stalks from fresh broccoli and most leaves. Put in boiling salted water, cook 15 minutes, drain, and keep hot. (Or cook frozen broccoli according to directions on packet; drain.)

Melt butter in pan, stir in flour, cook 1 minute. Remove from heat, gradually add reserved liquid, blend well. Return to heat, stir until sauce boils and thickens. Stir in whipped cream and sherry; season with salt and pepper.

Chicken and Almonds, one of the most popular of all Chinese chicken dishes. *See page 13.*

Arrange broccoli over base of ovenproof dish, pour half the sauce over. Arrange chicken pieces over sauce. Add parmesan cheese to remaining sauce, pour over chicken. Sprinkle with a little extra parmesan cheese.

Cook, uncovered, in moderate oven 15 to 20 minutes.

Serves 4.

Chicken Cordon Bleu

2 whole chicken breasts
2 slices gruyère cheese
2 thin slices ham
1 egg
1 tablespoon milk
packaged dry breadcrumbs
60 g (2 oz.) butter
1 tablespoon oil

Remove meat from bones in one piece from half the breasts at a time. Pound each piece until thin but still whole. Top two half breasts with slice of ham and slice of gruyère cheese. Top with remaining half breasts; secure on each side with small wooden sticks. Dip in mixture of beaten egg and milk, then press breadcrumbs on firmly. Refrigerate 1 hour to set the crumbs.

Heat butter and oil in pan. Cook chicken, turning occasionally, until tender, approximately 30 minutes. Drain well, remove small wooden sticks.

Serve with green salad. If desired, Mushroom Sauce can be offered separately.

Mushroom Sauce:

220 g can sliced mushrooms
½ cup cream
1 tablespoon dry sherry
salt, pepper

Sauce: Heat undrained mushrooms in small saucepan. Stir in cream and sherry. Season to taste with salt and pepper.

Serves 2.

Chicken Chop Suey

2 kg (4 lb.) chicken pieces
1 small green cabbage
½ small bunch celery
280 g can bean sprouts
1 onion
250 g (8 oz.) carrots
250 g (8 oz.) green beans
oil
2 tablespoons soy sauce
2 tablespoons cornflour
water
salt

Steam or boil chicken pieces until tender, cool; remove meat from bones, cut into large dice. Reserve stock in which chickens were cooked.

Shred cabbage, slice celery and carrots. String beans, cut in two or three pieces diagonally, chop onions. Heat oil in large saucepan, add vegetables, sauté until just tender but still crisp, season with salt.

Add chicken pieces; add reserved chicken stock to almost cover, add drained bean sprouts. Reheat gently, stir in soy sauce. Add cornflour blended with a little cold water; stir until mixture boils and thickens. Serves 6.

Chicken Chow Mein

1.5 kg (3 lb.) chicken
250 g (8 oz.) lean pork
½ cabbage
3 shallots
2 to 3 sticks celery
1 green pepper
1½ teaspoons soy sauce
250 g (½ lb.) prawns
1 teaspoon brandy or dry sherry
2 teaspoons cornflour
1 clove garlic
4 tablespoons oil
½ cup water
salt, pepper

Remove meat from uncooked chicken. Cut chicken meat and pork into fine shreds, place in bowl, sprinkle with salt. Add soy sauce, brandy, ½ teaspoon of the cornflour, and 1 teaspoon of oil; mix well.

Wash vegetables, cut into thin strips. Heat remaining oil in pan, add crushed garlic and chicken and pork mixture. Cook quickly 5 minutes, stirring constantly, sprinkle with pepper. Add prepared vegetables, cook until vegetables are tender, but still slightly crisp. Add shelled prawns. Mix remaining cornflour with water, add to pan, bring to boil, stirring gently.

Serve on top of crisp fried noodles.

Serves 4 to 6.

Crisp Fried Noodles: Drop 250 g (8 oz.) fine dried egg noodles into large saucepan of rapidly boiling salted water; stir with fork to separate, cook 3 to 4 minutes; drain well. Arrange a clean teatowel over wire cake cooler, spread noodles over this to drain. Leave at least 6 hours.

When ready to serve, drop noodles, a few at a time, into shallow hot oil. (To ensure thorough cooking, it is best to fry the noodles in 3 or 4 lots.) They cook in seconds; turn once during cooking.

Chicken Cacciatora

1.5 kg (3 lb.) chicken (or chicken pieces)
60 g (2 oz.) mushrooms
1 large onion
2 cloves garlic
1 tablespoon oil
440 g can whole tomatoes
1 bayleaf
½ cup red wine
salt, pepper

Slice mushrooms and onion, crush garlic. Joint chicken. Heat oil in pan, fry chicken pieces until golden brown. Remove from pan, drain well.

Add onion, mushrooms, and garlic to pan, sauté until tender. Return chicken pieces to pan, add tomatoes with their liquid, bayleaf, and wine, cook slowly, covered, 45 minutes, or until chicken is tender.

Season to taste with salt and pepper.

Serves 4.

Curried Chicken

1.5 kg (3 lb.)chicken pieces	1½ cups water
60 g (2 oz.) butter	2 medium onions
salt, pepper	pinch cayenne pepper
1¼ tablespoons curry powder	½ teaspoon paprika
½ cup tomato sauce	1 teaspoon cinnamon
	1 teaspoon allspice

Heat butter in pan, brown chicken well, remove from pan.

Add chopped onions, sauté until transparent. Add curry powder, cook a few minutes, add all remaining ingredients, bring to boil, stirring. Return chicken to pan, cover, reduce heat, simmer gently 50 minutes or until chicken is tender.

Serve with hot rice.

Serves 4.

Chicken en Cocotte

1.5 kg (3 lb.) chicken	2 sticks celery
500 g (1 lb.) small white onions	60 g (2 oz.) mushrooms
60 g (2 oz.) bacon pieces	30 g (1 oz.) butter
1 carrot	salt, pepper

Heat butter in pan, add whole chicken, cook until well browned all over; remove from pan, place in deep ovenproof dish.

Peel onions, leave whole, chop carrot and celery into 2.5 cm (1 in.) pieces, slice mushrooms. Add onions, carrot, celery and bacon pieces to pan, sauté until lightly golden, place in dish around chicken. Cover, bake in moderate oven 1 hour, add mushrooms, season with salt and pepper, cover, bake further 30 minutes, or until chicken is tender.

Serves 4.

Chicken Fricassee

1.5 kg (3 lb.) chicken (or chicken pieces)	3 shallots
60 g (2 oz.) butter	salt, pepper
1 clove garlic	125 g (4 oz.) mushrooms
1 cup dry white wine	30 g (1 oz.) butter extra
1½ cups water	½ cup milk
2 chicken stock cubes	2 tablespoons flour
	¼ cup cream

Cut chicken into serving-sized pieces, sauté in butter until light brown on all sides. Add crushed garlic, wine, water, crumbled stock cubes, chopped shallots, salt and pepper; cover and cook gently until chicken is tender. Melt extra butter in separate saucepan, sauté sliced mushrooms 3 minutes; drain. When chicken is tender, remove from pan.

Blend flour with milk, add gradually to pan, stir until sauce boils and thickens.

Return chicken pieces to pan, add mushrooms, reheat gently; season with salt and pepper. Just before serving, stir in cream.

Serves 4.

Chicken in a Basket

This is one of the most popular chicken dishes, particularly for a small, informal party.

Allow one small chicken 750 g to 1 kg (1½lb. to 2lb.) for each person; roast in usual way. Serve in small basket, lined with paper napkin. Packaged potato crisps (heat them in oven first) and fried onion rings are the correct accompaniments.

Chicken in the Basket is finger food, so serve finger bowls filled with warm water, with a slice of lemon floating in the water. As the water cools, the lemon can be used to remove any grease from fingers.

There's a correct way to eat this dish; Break off one leg first. Eat this before breaking off any further pieces. In this way the chicken retains its heat.

One hand only should be used to convey the food to the mouth. Rinse fingers often in the finger bowl. Make sure the dinner napkins are a good big size.

Chicken in Cream Sauce

1.5 kg (3 lb.) chicken pieces	½ teaspoon sugar
½ cup flour	½ cup cream
salt, pepper	1 tablespoon chopped parsley
125 g (4 oz.) butter	paprika
1 clove garlic	
½ cup dry white wine	

Roll chicken pieces in flour seasoned with salt and pepper. Melt butter in pan, fry crushed garlic 1 minute; add chicken, cook until golden brown on all sides.

Place chicken into greased casserole.

Add wine, salt, pepper, and sugar to pan drippings, bring to boil, stirring; pour over chicken.

Cover, bake in moderate oven 35 minutes or until chicken is tender.

Stir cream into casserole, blend well; cook further 10 minutes, uncovered.

Sprinkle top lightly with paprika and chopped parsley.

Serves 4.

Chicken in Nectar

1.5 kg (3 lb.) chicken pieces
1 packet onion soup
425 ml can apricot nectar
salt, pepper

Combine chicken pieces, onion soup, apricot nectar, salt, and pepper in casserole dish. Cover, cook in a moderate oven for 1½ hours or until chicken is tender.

Serve with rice.

Serves 4.

Chicken in Vermouth

1.5 kg (3 lb.) chicken (or chicken pieces)
2 onions
60 g (2 oz.) butter
1 clove garlic
1 tablespoon flour
¾ cup sweet vermouth
1 cup water
1 chicken stock cube
¼ cup vinegar
salt, pepper
1 teaspoon mixed herbs
60 g (2 oz.) black olives

Chop onions. Cut chicken into joints. Melt butter in saucepan, brown chicken on all sides; place in casserole.

Add onions and crushed garlic to pan, sauté until brown, stir in flour, cook 1 minute. Gradually add vermouth, water, vinegar; add crumbled stock cube. Return to heat; cook, stirring, until mixture boils and thickens. Season to taste with salt and pepper, add mixed herbs. Pour over chicken pieces.

Cook, covered, in moderate oven 1½ hours or until chicken is tender. Add olives 15 minutes before end of cooking time.

Serves 4.

Chicken in White Wine ✓

2 whole chicken breasts
flour
60 g (2 oz.) butter
1 cup dry white wine
salt, pepper
1 chicken stock cube
1 cup cream
2 teaspoons brandy

Remove bones carefully from whole chicken breasts, flatten out, and cut each in two. Dust with flour seasoned with salt and pepper; melt butter in pan, sauté gently about 5 minutes on each side.

Pour excess butter from pan, increase heat, and add wine. Cook quickly until wine is reduced by half, then reduce heat, add cream, and cook gently, uncovered, until sauce is reduced and chicken tender. Add crumbled stock cube, brandy, and salt to taste.

Arrange on heated serving dishes, sprinkle with a little paprika.

Serves 2.

Chicken Kiev

2 x 1.4 kg (2¾ lb.) chickens
185 g (6 oz.) butter
¼ cup milk
2 eggs
packaged dry breadcrumbs
salt
oil for deep frying

To fillet chicken: Lay bird on its back. Remove skin from breast and, with very sharp knife, cut out the white meat, including top section of the wing with the bone as far down as the joint. Lift out small fillet carefully. Remove any sinews, pound fillet gently to about 5 mm (¼ in.) thickness. Be careful not to separate meat from wingbone.

One chicken will give 2 fillets; remainder of bird can be used for soup or other dishes.

In the centre of each fillet put strip of cold butter about 5 cm (2 in.) long and 2 cm (¾ in.) thick. It is essential that butter be kept refrigerated until the moment of using, so that it is cold and hard; it is best to cut strips first and refrigerate them until needed.

Roll meat carefully round butter, with the wingbone sticking out like the stalk of a pear. It should look like a small lamb cutlet with the bone. Make sure butter is completely sealed in meat. Dip into eggs beaten with milk and salt, roll in breadcrumbs. Dip again in egg mixture, then in breadcrumbs.

Deep-fry in hot oil 7 to 10 minutes. (Cooking time will depend on size and thickness of chicken fillet.)

Serves 4.

Chicken Veronique—chicken in a rich, creamy sauce with green grapes. *See page 24.*

Chicken Marengo

1.5 kg (3 lb.) chicken pieces	1 cup chicken stock
2 tablespoons oil	salt, pepper
2 cloves garlic	¼ teaspoon mixed herbs
2 tablespoons flour	250 g (8 oz.) mushrooms
1½ cups dry white wine	½ cup chopped shallots
	3 tomatoes

Heat oil in pan, add crushed garlic and chicken pieces, brown chicken on all sides; remove from pan.

Stir flour into oil, cook a few minutes, then add wine and stock gradually; stir until mixture boils and thickens. Season with pepper, salt and mixed herbs, add sliced mushrooms, shallots and peeled, chopped tomatoes.

Cook for 5 minutes, then return chicken pieces to the pan, cover, simmer 45 minutes or until chicken is tender.

Serves 4.

Chicken Maryland

1.5 kg (3 lb.) chicken pieces	2 tablespoons milk
flour	packaged dry breadcrumbs
salt, pepper	oil for deep frying
1 egg	

Corn Fritters:

½ cup plain flour	¼ cup milk
½ cup self-raising flour	300 g can whole kernel corn
salt, pepper	oil for deep frying
1 egg, separated	

Fried Bananas:

4 bananas	butter
1 egg	
packaged dry breadcrumbs	

Beat egg and milk together. Toss chicken pieces in flour which has been seasoned with salt and pepper, dip in egg mixture, then toss in breadcrumbs.

Deep-fry in hot oil 5 to 10 minutes, or until chicken is pale golden colour, drain on absorbent paper. When ready to serve chicken, deep-fry again until golden brown.

Serve with fresh corn-on-the-cob or corn fritters, fried bananas, bacon rolls, and grilled tomatoes. *Note:* Frying the chicken pieces twice as above gives it a good crisp coating, and helps to retain moisture in the chicken.

Fried Bananas: Peel bananas, cut in half crosswise, dip in lightly beaten egg, then roll in breadcrumbs. Cook in heated butter until golden brown on all sides; drain well.

Corn Fritters: Sift flours, salt and pepper. Beat egg-yolk with milk; mix with drained corn, mix thoroughly into dry ingredients. Beat egg-white until soft peaks form, fold in.

Deep-fry dessertspoonfuls of mixture on hot oil until golden brown; drain.

Serves 4.

Chicken Mornay

2 kg (4 lb.) chicken pieces	1 onion
water	salt, pepper

Sauce:

125 g (4 oz.) butter	300 g can whole kernel corn
2 onions	385 g can whole mushrooms
3 sticks celery	90 g (3 oz.)grated cheese
⅔ cup flour	2 cups fresh breadcrumbs
1½ cups milk	60 g (2 oz.) butter, extra
salt, pepper	
½ cup sour cream	
½ cup dry white wine	

Put chicken pieces into large saucepan, add water to cover. Add salt, pepper, and chopped onion. Simmer, covered, 1¼ to 1½ hours or until chicken is tender. Remove chicken from stock and allow to cool. Strain stock and remove excess fat; reserve 1½ cups of stock for sauce (make up quantity with water, if necessary).

Remove chicken meat from bones, discarding skin; cut in serving-size pieces.

Sauce: Melt half the butter in saucepan, sauté chopped onions and sliced celery until transparent. Remove onion and celery from pan. Add remaining butter to pan. When hot, add flour, stir over heat 2 minutes; remove from heat. Gradually add milk and reserved stock, stir until smooth; return to heat, continue stirring until sauce boils and thickens. Add salt, pepper, sour cream and white wine. Stir in sautéed onion and celery, chicken pieces, drained corn, drained mushrooms and 30 g (1 oz.) grated cheese. Melt extra butter in saucepan, add breadcrumbs, mix well.

Pour chicken mixture into large greased ovenproof serving dish, sprinkle with remaining cheese, and top with buttered crumbs. Bake in moderate oven 25 to 30 minutes.

Serves 6.

Chicken Paprika

1.5 kg (3 lb.) chicken or chicken pieces)
salt, pepper
60 g (2 oz.) butter
2 onions
1 small green pepper
1 tomato
1 tablespoon tomato paste
1 tablespoon paprika
1 cup water
1 chicken stock cube
½ cup sour cream

Joint chicken, season with salt and pepper. Melt butter in large frying pan, add chicken pieces, cook until golden brown on both sides. Add finely chopped onions, pepper, paprika and peeled, chopped tomato. Continue cooking, covered, until vegetables and chicken are tender.

Remove chicken from pan, keep hot. Add tomato paste, water and stock cube to pan, blend well. Strain mixture, pressing vegetables through sieve as much as possible; return liquid to heat, add chicken, bring to boil; reduce heat, add sour cream, reheat without boiling.

Season to taste with salt and pepper.

Serves 4.

Chicken Pie

1.5 kg (3 lb.) chicken pieces
60 g (2 oz.) butter
4 tablespoons flour
2 tablespoons cream
125 g (4 oz.) mushrooms
3 shallots
1 tablespoon chopped parsley
½ red pepper
30 g (1 oz.) butter, extra
2 hard-boiled eggs
375 g packaged puff pastry
1 egg for glazing

Steam or boil chicken pieces in usual way until tender, reserve 2 cups of the stock. Remove skin and bones from chicken, chop meat into 2.5 cm (1 in.) pieces.

Melt butter in saucepan, remove from heat, add flour stir until smooth, add reserved liquid; stir well. Return to heat, bring to boil, stirring constantly. Reduce heat, simmer 2 to 3 minutes; remove from heat, add cream. Melt extra butter in frying pan, add sliced mushrooms, chopped shallots and red pepper. Sauté 3 to 4 minutes. Add to sauce with parsely and chicken. Allow to cool completely.

Place filling into 20 cm or 23 cm (8 in. or 9 in.) pie dish, top with sliced hard boiled eggs.

Roll out pastry to cover top of pie dish; dampen edge of pie dish with beaten egg. Carefully place pastry in position on top of pie, trim and flake edges. Glaze with beaten egg, decorate if desired.

Bake in very hot oven 10 minutes; reduce heat to moderately hot, cook further 10 to 15 minutes.

Serves 4 to 6.

Chicken Provencale

1.5 kg (3 lb.) chicken pieces
flour
salt, pepper
125 g (4 oz.) butter
1 medium onion
1 clove garlic
½ cup dry sherry
440 g can tomato purée
60 g (2 oz.) black olives
chopped parsley

Roll chicken pieces in flour seasoned with salt and pepper. Heat butter in frying pan, add chicken pieces, sauté until golden on all sides; transfer to casserole.

Add chopped onion and crushed garlic to remaining butter in frying pan, cook slowly until soft. Add sherry to pan, boil 1 minute, add tomato purée, stir until boiling, add salt and pepper to taste, pour over chicken.

Cover, bake in moderate oven 1 hour or until chicken is tender.

Add black olives and sprinkle with chopped parsley just before serving.

Serves 4.

Chicken Satay

1.5 kg (3 lb.) chicken
1 tablespoon ground cumin
2 tablespoons ground coriander
2 teaspoons sugar
½ teaspoon salt
1 teaspoon saffron

Satay Sauce:

1 onion
1 tablespoon oil
½ cup water
2 tablespoons peanut butter
½ teaspoon chilli powder
pinch salt
1 teaspoon sugar
1 teaspoon soy sauce
2 teaspoons lemon juice

Remove chicken meat from bones, cut into 2.5 cm (1 in.) cubes. Marinate chicken overnight with remaining ingredients.

Thread meat on to greased bamboo skewers. Grill, turning skewers occasionally, until cooked through; baste with oil or melted butter several times during grilling to keep moist.

Serve with Satay Sauce.

Satay Sauce: Sauté chopped onion in hot oil until soft. Add remaining ingredients; stir until sauce boils.

Serves 4.

Chicken Tandoori

1.5 kg (3 lb.) chicken pieces (or chicken drumsticks)
60 g (2 oz.) butter

Marinade:

1 cup yoghurt
1 teaspoon ground ginger
1 clove garlic
1 teaspoon garam masala
1 teaspoon salt

Crush garlic and mix into the yoghurt with spices and salt. Joint chicken and marinate in yoghurt mixture for 6 hours or overnight. Melt butter in baking dish, add drained chicken pieces.

Bake uncovered in moderate oven 45 minutes to 1 hour, basting occasionally with the yoghurt marinade.

Serve with chopped onion and lemon wedges.

Serves 4 to 6.

Chicken Tetrazzini

1.5 kg (3 lb.) chicken
1 onion
1 bayleaf
few bacon rinds or pieces
salt, pepper
60 g (2 oz.) butter
3 tablespoons flour
375 g (12 oz.) spaghetti
125 g (4 oz.) button mushrooms
30 g (1 oz.) butter, extra
1 cup cream
1 tablespoon dry sherry

Place chicken in pan with enough water to just cover chicken. Add peeled and roughly chopped onion, bayleaf, bacon, salt and pepper. Cover, bring to boil, reduce heat, simmer 1 hour, or until chicken is tender; remove from pan. Strain stock, reserve 1½ cups stock.

Remove meat from chicken bones, cut into thin strips. Add spaghetti to large quantity of boiling salted water, boil rapidly, uncovered 10 to 15 minutes, or until tender; drain.

Melt butter in saucepan, remove from heat, stir in flour, return to heat, stir constantly 2 minutes. Remove from heat, gradually stir in reserved stock. Return to heat, stir constantly until mixture boils and thickens. Add chicken, cream and sherrry, reheat without boiling. Add sliced mushrooms, which have been sautéed in extra butter.

Serve over hot spaghetti.

Serves 4 to 6.

Chinese Lemon Chicken

1.5 kg (3 lb.) chicken (or chicken pieces)
60 g (2 oz.) butter

Lemon Sauce:

½ cup bottled lemon sauce
2 tablespoons sweet sherry
2 to 3 tablespoons water

Put chicken or chicken pieces in baking dish, brush with melted butter, cook in moderate oven until tender, approximately 1¼ hours.

Remove to serving dishes, pour hot Lemon Sauce over.

Place lemon sauce in small saucepan. Add sherry and enough water to mix to desired consistency, stir until boiling.

Serves 4.

Note: The Chinese lemon sauce is available in jars from Chinese food stores.

Crusty Chicken Wings

1 kg (2 lb.) chicken wings
oil
1 cup packaged dry breadcrumbs
salt, pepper
½ teaspoon oregano
1 teaspoon curry powder

Combine breadcrumbs, salt, pepper, oregano and curry powder in plastic bag. Dip chicken wings in oil; add half-dozen chicken wings at a time to bag; seal bag and shake well to coat evenly. Continue until all wings have been done. Place on sheet of aluminuim foil in baking dish, bake in moderate oven 35 minutes or until tender.

Serves 4 to 6.

Chicken Souffle

1.25 kg (2½ lb.) chicken pieces
2 cups milk
1 small bayleaf
1 small onion
pinch ground thyme
60 g (2 oz.) butter
⅓ cup flour
pinch nutmeg
salt, pepper
3 eggs

Steam or boil chicken pieces in usual way until tender. Remove meat from bones; discard skin. Chop meat roughly.

Place milk, bayleaf, chopped onion and thyme in saucepan, bring slowly to boil, remove from heat, stand 10 minutes; strain, reserve liquid. Melt butter in pan, add flour, cook 1 minute. Remove from heat, gradually add reserved liquid. Return to heat, stir until sauce boils and thickens. Place sauce and chicken in electric blender, blend until smooth (or chop chicken very finely, add to sauce). Add nutmeg, and salt and pepper to taste. Separate eggs, add egg-yolks to chicken mixture, blend well. Fold in softly beaten egg-whites. Pour mixture into lightly greased 1 litre (2-pint) soufflé dish. Bake in moderately hot oven 20 minutes. Serve immediately.

Serves 4.

Oven-Fried Lemon Chicken—butter and a lemon sauce are poured over the chicken while it cooks, to make it beautifully moist, deliciously succulent. *See page 33.*

Chicken Veronique

1.5 kg (3 lb.) chicken pieces
30 g (1 oz.) butter
1 tablespoon flour
1 cup water
1 chicken stock cube
¼ cup brandy
½ cup cream
125 g (4 oz.) small white grapes
salt, pepper

Heat butter in pan, add chicken pieces, cook until golden brown; stir in flour; add water, stock cube, and brandy, cover, simmer 30 minutes, or until chicken is tender.

Season with salt and pepper, add cream and grapes, reheat gently without boiling.

Serves 4.

Note: When grapes are out of season, canned grapes can be used.

Chicken Vol-au-vent

1.5 kg (3 lb.) chicken
water
salt, pepper
6 peppercorns
1 bayleaf
60 g (2 oz.) butter
1 small onion
250 g button mushrooms
⅓ cup flour
300 g can asparagus soup
1 tablespoon dry sherry
6 10 cm (4 in.) vol-au-vent cases
chopped parsley

Place chicken in saucepan with water to cover. Add salt, peppercorns, and bayleaf. Bring to boil, reduce heat, simmer, covered, 45 minutes or until tender. Strain, reserve 1½ cups of stock.

Bone chicken, cut meat into large cubes or pieces.

Melt butter in separate pan, sauté chopped onion and sliced mushrooms a few minutes. Stir in flour, cook a few minutes. Remove from heat, gradually add reserved stock. Return to heat, stir until sauce boils and thickens. Add undiluted soup and sherry. Add chicken pieces, reheat gently. Season to taste with salt and pepper. Spoon into vol-au-vent cases. Heat in hot oven 5 minutes. Sprinkle with parsley. Makes 6.

Chicken with Marsala

1.5 kg (3 lb.) chicken pieces
30 g (1 oz.) butter
425 ml can tomato juice
1½ tablespoons cornflour
¼ cup marsala
½ cup water
2 teaspoons worcestershire sauce
salt, pepper

Put chicken pieces in single layer, skin side up, into large ovenproof dish; brush with melted butter. Blend cornflour and tomato juice together, add remaining ingredients; mix well. Pour sauce over chicken.

Bake uncovered, in moderate oven 1 hour, or until chicken is tender. Spoon sauce over chicken frequently during cooking. Serves 4.

Chicken with Orange

2 x 1.4 kg (2¾ lb.) chickens
125 g (4 oz.) butter
salt, pepper

Orange Sauce:

3 oranges
1 tablespoon sugar
2 teaspoons vinegar
2 cups chicken stock or water
2 teaspoons lemon juice
3 teaspoons arrowroot
½ cup sweet sherry
¼ cup grand marnier or other orange liqueur
salt, pepper

Cut chickens in half, place cut side down in baking dish, spread with softened butter, season with salt and pepper. Bake in moderate oven 45 minutes to 1 hour, or until chickens are golden brown and tender. Serve with Orange Sauce spooned over.

Orange Sauce: Remove rind from one orange, using vegetable peeler. Cut rind into thin strips. Drop into boiling water, boil 3 minutes; drain. This removes bitterness from the skin. Squeeze and strain juice from the three oranges.

Strain pan drippings from chicken, skim off any fat, reserve pan drippings. Place sugar and vinegar into dish, cook over heat, without stirring, until sugar turns light golden brown. Add reserved pan drippings, stock, orange juice and rind and lemon juice. Boil rapidly until sauce is reduced by half. Blend arrowroot with sherry, stir into sauce, stir until mixture boils and thickens. Season with salt and pepper, stir in orange liqueur.

Serves 4.

Chicken Saute Chasseur

1.5 kg (3 lb.) chicken (or chicken pieces)
salt, pepper
60 g (2 oz.) butter
1 tablespoon oil
125 g (4 oz.) mushrooms
1 medium onion
2 tablespoons brandy
½ cup dry white wine
1 cup water
1 chicken stock cube
2 tomatoes
15 g (½ oz.) butter extra
2 teaspoons flour
2 tablespoons tomato paste
2 tablespoons chopped parsley

Joint chicken, season with salt and pepper. Heat butter and oil in large frying pan. Add chicken, sauté until evenly browned; cover, reduce heat, continue cooking 10 minutes, remove from pan.

Add sliced mushrooms and finely chopped onion to pan, sauté 3 minutes; remove from pan. Add to pan—brandy, wine, stock cube, water, and peeled and chopped tomatoes. Bring to boil; cook, uncovered, until sauce is reduced by half.

Blend extra butter with flour, add to sauce with tomato paste; stir constantly, until mixture boils and thickens. Add chicken, cover, simmer 25 minutes or until tender. Add mushrooms, onion, and parsley, heat thoroughly. Serves 4.

Chicken with Peaches

1.5 kg (3 lb.) chicken (or chicken pieces)
½ cup flour
salt, pepper
125 g (4 oz.) butter
2 large potatoes
125 g (4 oz.) bacon
125 g (4 oz.) mushrooms
2 onions
1 tablespoon flour, extra
6 shallots
425 g can peach slices or halves
1½ cups water
1 chicken stock cube
chopped parsley

Joint chicken, coat pieces with flour seasoned with salt and pepper. Dice bacon, slice mushrooms, onions, and shallots. Melt butter in pan, fry chicken until golden brown and tender; keep hot. Meanwhile, peel and dice potatoes, cook in salted water until tender but still firm; drain.

Add bacon to butter in which chicken was cooked, add onions and mushrooms, cook gently until onions are soft. If desired, the potatoes can also be added and sautéed until golden. Stir in extra flour, remove from heat, and gradually add water; add crumbled stock cube. Return to heat; cook, stirring, until mixture boils and thickens. Add potatoes (if not added earlier) and shallots, heat through gently.

Put undrained peaches in pan, heat through; drain. Arrange chicken on serving plate, arrange peaches round, spoon sauce over. Sprinkle with chopped parsley. Serves 4 to 6.

Chicken-Pineapple Casserole

1.5 kg (3 lb.) chicken (or chicken pieces)
1 onion
125 g (4 oz.) bacon
125 g (4 oz.) mushrooms
2 tablespoons flour
450 g can pineapple pieces
60 g (2 oz.) butter
flour, extra
salt, pepper
1 cup water
1 chicken stock cube
chopped parsley

Cut chicken into serving sized pieces. Toss in flour seasoned with salt and pepper.

Cut rind from bacon rashers. Divide each rasher into 3 pieces; roll each piece into a small roll and secure with a wooden stick. Slice onion and mushrooms

Melt butter, sauté onion lightly, remove from pan. Add bacon rolls, cook until well browned. Remove from pan. Fry chicken pieces until well browned on all sides, remove from pan. Add 2 tablespoons flour to pan and cook until brown (do not burn). Slowly stir in the water. Add crumbled stock cube. Bring to boil, stirring.

Put mushrooms, onion, and chicken in oven-proof dish. Pour sauce over. Arrange drained pineapple pieces and bacon rolls (with wooden sticks removed) on top.

Cover, bake in moderate oven 1 to 1¼ hours until chicken is tender.

Serve in deep bowls with hot rice. Sprinkle with chopped parsley.

Serves 4.

Chicken with Oyster Sauce

1.5 kg (3 lb.) chicken pieces
water
2 carrots
2 onions
1 stick celery
1 bayleaf
½ teaspoon ground thyme
salt

Oyster Sauce:

60 g (2 oz.) butter
4 shallots
¼ cup flour
1 to 2 bottles oysters
1 chicken stock cube
2 teaspoons white wine
½ cup cream
salt, pepper
chopped parsley

Place chicken pieces in saucepan, cover with cold water. Add peeled and halved carrots and onions, celery, parsley, bayleaf, thyme, salt. Bring to boil, skim well . Reduce heat, cover, simmer ¾ hour or until tender.

Arrange chicken pieces in serving dish. Pour Oyster Sauce over. Sprinkle with chopped parsley.

Oyster Sauce: Drain oysters. Measure oyster liquid and add enough strained stock from chicken to make 1½ cups. Poach oysters in this liquid over low heat for a few minutes until edges curl. Drain oysters, reserving liquid.

Melt butter in saucepan, add chopped shallots, cook 4 minutes. Stir in flour, cook further 2 minutes. Remove from heat, gradually add reserved liquid and wine. Return to heat, bring to boil, stirring; reduce heat, stir for further 2 to 3 minutes. Add crumbled stock cube, cream, salt and pepper to taste. Add oysters, heat through gently.

Serves 4.

Chicken Teriyaki

8 chicken drumsticks

Marinade:

2 tablespoons soy sauce
½ cup lemon juice
1 clove crushed garlic
½ teaspoon salt
1 teaspoon grated green ginger
½ cup canned pineapple juice

Combine all ingredients for marinade; add chicken legs, marinate for 2 hours.

Remove chicken legs from marinade, place in greased baking dish, spoon over 2 tablespoons of marinade. Bake, uncovered, in moderate oven 45 minutes or until tender.

Serve with hot rice.

Serves 4.

Chicken with Pineapple

1.5 kg (3 lb.) chicken
1 onion
1 carrot
2 sticks celery
30 g (1 oz.) butter
450 g can pineapple pieces
salt, pepper
1 packet cream of chicken soup
2 teaspoons soy sauce
1 tablespoon vinegar

Place chicken in large saucepan, cover with water, season with salt and pepper, bring to boil, cover, reduce heat, simmer 1 hour, or until chicken is tender.

Remove chicken from pan, allow to cool, strain stock, reserve 3 cups stock. Remove chicken meat from bones, chop roughly.

Peel and slice onion and carrot, chop celery. Melt butter in frying pan, add vegetables, sauté until tender, but not brown, add chicken, contents of soup packet, reserved stock, undrained pineapple, then remaining ingredients, mix well, cover, cook 20 minutes.

Serve with hot rice.

Serves 4.

Chinese Chicken Omelet

8 eggs
500 g (1 lb.) cooked chicken
6 shallots
2 sticks celery
60 g (2 oz.) mushrooms
280 g can bean sprouts
salt, pepper
2 tablespoons oil

Sauce:

1 cup water
2 chicken stock cubes
1 teaspoon sugar
1 tablespoon cornflour
2 teaspoons soy sauce
¼ cup cold water

Chop mushrooms, cook in 1 teaspoon of hot oil until tender; drain, set aside. Chop shallots and celery finely. Cut chicken into fine strips.

Beat eggs lightly as for omelet. Add chicken, shallots, celery, mushrooms, and drained bean sprouts. Add seasonings and mix lightly.

Heat remaining oil in frypan, pour in enough omelet mixture to make small omelets about 12 cm (5 in.) in diameter. (Several can cook at the same time.) When firm on one side, turn, cook other side. Stack on warm plate while cooking remainder of omelets; keep warm.

To serve, stack 3 omelets on top of each other; spoon sauce over.

Sauce: Combine cornflour with cold water. Put remaining ingredients in small saucepan, bring to boil. Stir in blended cornflour. Cook, stirring, until sauce boils and thickens.

Serves 4.

Coq au Vin

2 kg (4 lb.) chicken pieces
60 g (2 oz.) butter
125 g (¼ lb.) bacon pieces
12 tiny onions
salt, pepper
250 g (½ lb.) mushrooms
1 clove garlic
½ cup flour
2½ cups chicken stock or water
⅓ cup brandy
1½ cups dry red wine
¼ teaspoon thyme
½ teaspoon mixed herbs
1 bayleaf
60 g (2 oz.) butter, extra

Heat butter in heavy pan, add diced bacon and peeled onions. Cook a few minutes, remove from pan. Add chicken pieces to pan drippings, brown well, remove from pan. Add sliced mushrooms and crushed garlic to pan, cook a few minutes, remove.

Add extra butter to pan drippings; when melted, stir in flour, stir until golden brown. Remove from heat, gradually add stock, blend well. Return to heat, stir until sauce boils and thickens. Add brandy and wine, thyme, herbs and bayleaf. Return chicken and vegetables to pan, bring to boil, reduce heat, simmer, covered, 30 minutes or until tender. Season to taste with salt and pepper. (If preferred, bake in moderate oven, covered, 40 minutes or until tender.)

Serve with hot garlic bread and tossed green salad.

Serves 6.

Chicken Newburg

1.5 kg (3 lb.) chicken
30 g (1 oz.) butter
salt, pepper
¾ cup dry sherry
1 cup cream
2 egg-yolks
chopped parsley

Steam or boil chicken until tender; drain (the chicken stock can be used as basis for soup, or in another recipe).

Bone chicken, cut meat into large bite-size pieces. Melt butter in pan, add chicken, sauté 2 minutes, do not brown. Season with salt and pepper. Add sherry, simmer slowly until almost all sherry has been reduced. Beat egg-yolks and cream together, pour over chicken, shake or stir gently over low heat until sauce thickens slightly; do not boil. Sprinkle with parsley. Serve with rice.

Serves 4.

Coq au Vin—deliciously rich combination of chicken, mushrooms, bacon, onions, cooked in red wine and brandy.

Creamy Chicken Casserole

1.5 kg (3 lb.) chicken
60 g (2 oz.) butter
2 tablespoons flour
salt, pepper
440 g can cream of chicken soup
½ cup cream
2 tablespoons finely chopped parsley
2 sticks celery
440 g can whole kernel corn
1 cup fresh breadcrumbs
30 g (1 oz.) butter extra

Boil chicken in usual way, until tender; reserve 1 cup of the chicken stock.

Heat butter in large saucepan, add flour, cook 2 minutes. Remove from heat, gradually add reserved chicken stock. Return to heat, bring to boil stirring; reduce heat, simmer, uncovered, 2 minutes. Season with salt and pepper. Add undiluted soup, cream and finely chopped parsley; mix well. Remove chicken meat from bones, chop roughly, add to sauce with chopped celery, and drained corn; mix lightly. Pour into ovenproof dish.

Melt extra butter in frying pan, add breadcrumbs; toss lightly. Sprinkle crumbs over chicken.

Bake, uncovered, in moderate oven 25 minutes, or until heated through and golden brown.

Serves 6.

Creole Chicken Gumbo

1.5 kg (3 lb.) chicken pieces
½ cup oil
2 medium onions
2 tablespoons flour
1 clove garlic
140 g can tomato paste
2½ cups water
2 chicken stock cubes
salt, pepper
2 teaspoons lemon juice
½ teaspoon ground thyme
2 sticks celery
6 shallots
1 green pepper
1 red pepper
500 g (1 lb.) prawns
½ cup chopped parsley

Heat oil in pan, add chicken pieces; cook, turning occasionally, until chicken is well browned on all sides. Remove from pan.

Add chopped onions and crushed garlic to pan, sauté until transparent. Stir in flour; cook, stirring, until flour is lightly golden. Stir in water, crumbled stock cubes and tomato paste, mix well; stir until sauce boils. Reduce heat, return chicken to pan, add salt, pepper, thyme and lemon juice. Cook, covered, 30 minutes.

Add chopped celery, shallots and peppers; simmer further 10 to 15 minutes or until tender. Add shelled prawns, heat through.

Sprinkle with chopped parsley.

Serves 6.

Curried Chicken Legs

8 chicken drumsticks approx. 1 kg (2 lb.)
salt, pepper
¼ teaspoon paprika
1 cup water
2 chicken stock cubes
¼ cup dry white wine
2 teaspoons curry powder
125 g (4 oz.) mushrooms
1 onion

Place chicken legs under griller, grill on both sides until golden brown; place in ovenproof dish. Combine salt, pepper, paprika, water, crumbled stock cubes, wine, curry powder, sliced mushrooms and peeled and finely chopped onion in a bowl; mix well, then pour over chicken legs.

Cover, bake in moderate oven 30 minutes, remove cover, bake further 20 minutes or until chicken is tender.

Serves 4.

Delicious Curried Chicken

1.5 kg (3 lb.) chicken pieces
125 g (4 oz.) butter
2 onions
1 clove garlic
1 teaspoon turmeric
pinch chilli powder
1½ cups water
½ teaspoon ground ginger
1 teaspoon ground coriander
salt
1 chicken stock cube
250 g (8 oz.) button mushrooms
2 zucchini
4 shallots

Heat butter in pan. Add finely chopped onions and crushed garlic, sauté a few minutes. Add turmeric, chilli powder, ginger, coriander, and salt, cook 2 minutes. Add chicken pieces, fry until golden brown. Add water and crumbled stock cube. Cover and simmer 30 minutes or until chicken is tender.

Add halved mushrooms, sliced zucchini, and chopped shallots. Cook further 5 minutes.

Serve with hot rice.

Serves 4.

Devilled Chicken

8 chicken drumsticks
¾ cup tomato sauce
2 tablespoons worcestershire sauce
1 teaspoon dry mustard
1 clove garlic
½ cup water
1 chicken stock cube

Steam or bake chicken legs until tender.

Crush garlic, combine with remaining ingredients in saucepan. Bring to boil, reduce heat, simmer 5 minutes. Add chicken legs, continue cooking a further 5 minutes or until sauce has thickened slightly.

Serves 4.

Honeyed Chicken

1.5 kg (3 lb.) chicken (or chicken pieces)
90 g (3 oz.) butter

Sauce:

4 shallots
1 teaspoon finely chopped green ginger
1 tablespoon honey
1 tablespoon soy sauce
½ teaspoon salt
½ cup dry sherry

Melt butter in baking dish, add chicken, brush well with butter, bake in moderately hot oven 45 minutes; baste frequently with the butter. Pour sauce over chicken, continue cooking for further 30 minutes, or until tender and golden brown. Baste chicken frequently with sauce during last 30 minutes.

Sauce: Chop shallots finely, combine with remaining ingredients.

Serves 4.

Garlic-Lemon Chicken

1.5 kg (3 lb.) chicken pieces
1 clove garlic
1 teaspoon paprika
2 teaspoons soy sauce
¼ cup lemon juice
2 teaspoons grated lemon rind
salt, pepper

Arrange chicken pieces in single layer on large piece of aluminium foil. Combine crushed garlic with remaining ingredients, brush over chicken pieces. Wrap chicken pieces tightly in the foil. Place in pan of simmering water, cover tightly, simmer gently 45 minutes to 1 hour, or until chicken is tender.

Serves 4.

Hawaiian Chicken

2 kg (4 lb.) chicken pieces
¼ cup soy sauce
½ cup dry white wine
2 tablespoons lemon juice
1 clove garlic
½ teaspoon curry powder
½ teaspoon ground ginger
salt, pepper
125 g (4 oz.) butter
2 onions
flour
375 g (¾ lb.) rice
450 g can pineapple slices
30 g (1 oz.) butter, extra
½ cup toasted slivered almonds
1 red pepper

Mix together soy sauce, ¼ cup white wine, lemon juice, crushed garlic, curry powder and ginger.

Pour over chicken pieces, marinate several hours, turning occasionally. Melt butter in pan, sauté sliced onions until golden brown; remove from pan. Drain chicken, reserve marinade. Pat chicken dry, then coat lightly with flour which has been seasoned with salt and pepper.

Cook in pan until golden brown, turning occasionally. Add onions and reserved marinade; cover, simmer gently 45 minutes, or until tender, uncovering pan for last 15 minutes.

Meanwhile, boil rice in usual way, drain and keep hot. Cut pineapple slices in half and brown in extra butter; fry chopped pepper until softened.

To serve, mix rice, toasted almonds and red pepper. Heap on large platter. Arrange chicken pieces and pineapple slices over or around. Add remaining ¼ cup white wine to pan drippings, heat, stirring; pour over chicken.

Serves 6.

Imperial Chicken

1.5 kg (3 lb.) chicken
2 teaspoons honey
1 teaspoon soy sauce
1 tablespoon oil
3 sticks celery
1 onion
12 water chestnuts
1 cup water
1 chicken stock cube
2 teaspoons sugar
¼ cup vinegar
2 teaspoons soy sauce, extra
2 teaspoons cornflour
1 tablespoon water, extra
310 g can mandarin segments
1 tablespoon chopped parsley
¼ cup blanched toasted almonds

Place chicken on rack in baking dish, cook in moderate oven 1¼ hours, or until tender. Half an hour before it is done, brush skin well with mixture of honey and soy sauce. Return chicken to oven, and increase heat to hot. Cook until skin is crisp and golden. Joint chicken and keep warm.

Heat oil in frying pan, sauté sliced celery, sliced onion, and halved water chestnuts. Add water, crumbled stock cube, sugar, vinegar, and soy sauce. Blend cornflour with extra water and stir into pan; cook, stirring, until sauce boils and thickens. Add chicken pieces, cover, and cook until heated through.

Add parsley, transfer to serving dish, scatter over the mandarin sections which have been heated in their liquid, then drained. Sprinkle with almonds.

Serves 4.

Cream of Chicken Florentine

1 bunch young spinach
60 g (2 oz.) butter
1.5 kg (3 lb.) chicken
125 g (4 oz.) mushrooms
1 red pepper
60 g (2 oz.) butter, extra
salt, pepper
125 g (4 oz.) grated cheese

Sauce:

60 g (2 oz.) butter
½ cup flour
2 cups milk
¼ cup sour cream
salt, pepper

Topping:

30 g (1 oz.) butter
1 cup fresh breadcrumbs

Steam or boil chicken until tender; drain (the chicken stock can be used as a basis for soup, or in another recipe).

Wash spinach, remove hard, white stalks, chop leaves coarsely. Melt butter in pan, add spinach, sauté until tender; arrange over base of lightly greased ovenproof dish.

Remove meat from chicken, cut into 2.5 cm (1 in.) cubes, put on top of spinach. Slice mushrooms and pepper, sauté in extra butter until tender, arrange over chicken. Season with salt and pepper, top with sauce, cheese, and buttered breadcrumbs.

Bake in moderate oven 30 minutes, or until golden brown and well heated.

Sauce: Melt butter in saucepan, remove from heat, add flour, stir until smooth; return to heat, cook one minute, stirring constantly; remove from heat. Gradually stir in milk, return to heat, cook, stirring constantly until sauce boils and thickens; stir in sour cream.

Season to taste with salt and pepper.

Buttered Breadcrumbs: Melt butter in frying pan, add breadcrumbs, cook, stirring constantly, until golden brown.

Serves 4 to 6.

Herbed Chicken with Spaghetti

2 cloves garlic
4 tablespoons oil
1.5 kg (3 lb.) chicken pieces
1 teaspoon salt
440 g can whole tomatoes
¼ teaspoon oregano
¼ teaspoon basil
1 cup water
1 chicken stock cube
250 g (8 oz.) spaghetti or macaroni
1 tablespoon chopped parsley

Sauté crushed garlic in hot oil for 1 minute. Add chicken pieces, cook over moderate heat until chicken is brown on both sides. Pour off excess fat. Add chopped tomatoes and liquid from can, water, crumbled stock cube, salt, oregano, and basil; simmer, covered, 30 to 40 minutes, until chicken is tender, stirring occasionally.

Remove lid, cook rapidly for 5 minutes to thicken sauce.

Cook spaghetti in large saucepan of boiling salted water 12 minutes; drain.

Put pasta in serving dish, arrange chicken pieces down the centre, pour sauce over; sprinkle with parsley.

Serves 4.

Golden-Crumbed Chicken Rolls

4 large whole chicken breasts
3 eggs
flour
salt, pepper
packaged dry breadcrumbs
90 g (3 oz.) butter

Filling:

4 rashers bacon
250 g (8 oz.) mushrooms
4 shallots
1 medium onion
½ teaspoon thyme
salt, pepper
60 g (2 oz.) butter

Remove chicken breasts from bones (giving 8 individual pieces), pound each piece with mallet or rolling pin until very thin. Spread each chicken breast evenly with prepared filling, fold in sides, roll up, secure with small skewers. Roll in flour seasoned with salt and pepper, dip in beaten eggs, then breadcrumbs. Roll again in egg and breadcrumbs.

Melt butter in baking dish, add rolls, bake uncovered in moderate oven 35 to 40 minutes, turning rolls frequently.

Spoon over Bearnaise Sauce just before serving.

Lightly cooked zucchini and red cabbage are ideal accompaniments (the red cabbage obtainable in cans or jars can be used, just heat in its own liquid.)

Filling: Remove rind from bacon; chop bacon finely. Melt butter in frying pan, add bacon, chopped mushrooms, chopped shallots, peeled and finely chopped onion, thyme, salt, and pepper. Sauté until onion is transparent. Remove from heat.

Bearnaise Sauce:

4 tablespoons tarragon vinegar
1 shallot
1 bayleaf
6 peppercorns
3 egg-yolks
125 g (4 oz.) butter
salt, pepper

Boil vinegar, peppercorns, chopped shallot, and bayleaf together until liquid is reduced to 2 tablespoons; strain. Beat egg-yolks lightly in top of double saucepan, and stir in strained liquid. Gradually beat in cooled melted butter, and whisk continuously over simmering water until thickened. Season to taste with salt and pepper.

Serves 4.

Golden-Crumbed Chicken Rolls: double-crumbing gives crisp coating to these delicious chicken rolls, with a filling of bacon, mushrooms, thyme. Rich Bearnaise Sauce is spooned over.

Kenya Chicken Curry

1.5 kg (3 lb.) chicken pieces
60 g (2 oz.) butter
4 large onions
1 clove garlic
1 tablespoon tomato paste
½ cup water
¼ teaspoon chilli powder
¼ teaspoon turmeric
½ teaspoon ground ginger
1 teaspoon cinnamon
2 teaspoons curry powder
salt, pepper
2 tablespoons lemon juice
1 tablespoon milk

Heat butter in pan, add sliced onions, crushed garlic, and chicken pieces, cook until chicken is well browned. Add remaining ingredients; mix well. Simmer, covered, 1½ hours, or until chicken is tender.

Serve with hot rice.

Serves 4.

Lazy-Day Chicken

1.5 kg (3 lb.) chicken pieces
1 cup sour cream
440 g can cream of chicken soup
1 packet onion soup mix
½ cup water
1 packet crisp fried noodles

Put chicken pieces into deep ovenproof dish. Combine sour cream, chicken soup, onion soup and water in bowl. Pour over chicken. Cover, bake in moderate oven 1½ hours or until chicken is tender.

Sprinkle crisp noodles or crushed potato chips over; cook uncovered, further 10 minutes.

Serves 4.

Indian Spiced Chicken

1.5 kg (3 lb.) chicken (or chicken pieces)
90 g (3 oz.) butter
¼ teaspoon ground ginger
½ teaspoon turmeric
¼ teaspoon ground cardamom
8 whole cloves
2.5 cm (1 in.) piece cinnamon stick
2 onions
½ clove garlic
¼ teaspoon chilli powder
1 teaspoon salt
2 tablespoons flour
1 cup water
2 chicken stock cubes

Joint chicken. Melt butter in large frying pan, add chicken pieces, turn in the melted butter until coated on all sides. Sprinkle over combined ginger, turmeric, cardamom, cloves, and cinnamon stick, which has been broken up into small pieces. Fry over medium heat until chicken is brown (12 to 15 minutes). Then add combined chopped onions, crushed garlic, and chilli powder; cover, cook over low heat 30 minutes or until chicken is tender.

Remove chicken from pan, remove whole cloves, discard. Add flour and salt to pan, blend well, cook 1 minute. Add water and crumbled stock cubes, stir until sauce boils and thickens.

Return chicken pieces to sauce, simmer over low heat 10 minutes.

Serves 4.

Mayonnaise-Chicken Casserole

2 kg (4 lb.) chicken pieces
1 cup rice
boiling salted water
1 large onion
440 g can cream of chicken soup
440 g can cream of mushroom soup
salt, pepper
4 sticks celery
1 cup mayonnaise
2 tablespoons lemon juice
½ cup fresh breadcrumbs
60 g (2 oz.) butter

Steam or boil chicken, cool; remove meat from bones, cut into large dice; discard skin. Cook rice in boiling salted water until tender, drain. Chop onions, dice celery. Sauté in 30 g (1 oz.) butter until transparent; drain. Combine all ingredients except breadcrumbs and remaining butter. Put mixture in large casserole, top with breadcrumbs which have been tossed in remaining melted butter.

Bake, uncovered, in moderate oven 30 minutes.

Serves 6.

Mexican Chicken

1.5 kg (3 lb.) chicken pieces
1 teaspoon salt
1 teaspoon paprika
½ cup oil
30 g (1 oz.) butter
1 teaspoon saffron
1 cup rice
3 cups chicken stock
1 bayleaf
1 red pepper
60 g (2 oz.) black olives
1 cup cooked green peas

Season chicken with salt and paprika. Heat oil, sauté chicken pieces until brown. Remove chicken from pan, drain off oil. Melt butter, add saffron and washed, uncooked rice. Cook a few minutes, stirring occasionally. Add stock, cover, simmer 10 minutes. Return chicken to pan, add bayleaf, chopped red pepper, and olives.

Cover, simmer 30 to 35 minutes or until chicken is tender. About 15 minutes before end of cooking time, add the peas, stir in gently.

Serves 4.

Oriental Chicken

1.5 kg (3 lb.) chicken (or chicken pieces)
⅓ cup cornflour
salt, pepper
¼ teaspoon ground ginger
¼ cup oil
3 sticks celery
1 red pepper
1 tablespoon cornflour, extra
1 tablespoon brown sugar
1 tablespoon vinegar
2 teaspoons soy sauce
450 g can pineapple pieces
½ cup water

Cut chicken into serving-sized pieces. Toss chicken in combined cornflour, salt, pepper, and ginger. Heat oil in large saucepan, add chicken pieces, brown well; reduce heat, cover, and cook 30 minutes or until chicken is tender.

Remove chicken from pan; keep hot. Add sliced celery and pepper to pan, sauté 3 minutes; pour off oil. Add to pan combined extra cornflour, brown sugar, vinegar, soy sauce, undrained pineapple pieces, and water. Bring to boil, stirring; reduce heat, simmer, uncovered, 3 minutes.

Place chicken pieces on serving dish, pour sauce over, garnish with fried walnuts.

Serve with boiled rice.

Fried Walnuts: Heat 1 tablespoon of oil in pan, add ⅓ cup of walnut halves or pieces, sauté 2 minutes. Drain on absorbent paper.

Serves 4.

Oven-fried Lemon Chicken

1.5 kg (3 lb.) chicken (or chicken pieces)
½ cup flour
1 teaspoon salt
¼ teaspoon pepper
2 teaspoons paprika
125 g (4 oz.) butter

Lemon Sauce:

2 teaspoons soy sauce
salt, pepper
¼ cup oil
⅓ cup lemon juice
2 teaspoons grated lemon rind
1 clove crushed garlic

Combine flour, salt, pepper, and paprika. Cut chicken into serving-sized pieces; toss in the seasoned flour. Grease large ovenproof dish, arrange chicken pieces, skin-side down, in single layer. Melt butter, spoon over chicken. Bake, uncovered, in hot oven 30 minutes, turn chicken, spoon over Lemon Sauce; return to oven, cook further 30 minutes, or until tender, basting occasionally.

Lemon Sauce: Combine all ingredients; mix well. Refrigerate 1 hour.

Serves 4.

Paella

500 g (1 lb.) long grain rice
3½ cups water
1 chicken stock cube
2 cloves garlic
1 tablespoon chopped parsley
1 teaspoon saffron
salt, pepper
60 g (2 oz.) butter
1 onion
1 green pepper
1 red pepper
2 whole chicken breasts
125 g (4 oz.) bacon pieces
400 g can artichoke hearts
250 g packet quick frozen peas
250 g (8 oz.) prawns
500 g-1 kg (1 lb.-2 lb.) mussels

Slice peppers into thin strips. Melt butter in large frying pan, add peppers. Sauté 2 to 3 minutes, remove from pan. Remove chicken breasts from bone, slice meat into approx. 5 cm (2 in.) pieces. Add sliced onion, chicken and chopped bacon pieces to pan, brown lightly on all sides. Add halved artichoke hearts, peas, rice, water, crumbled chicken stock cube, crushed garlic, parsley, salt, pepper, and saffron; mix well. Cover, simmer gently for 20 minutes or until rice is tender and fluffy.

While rice is cooking scrub mussel shells well under cold running water. Put in large saucepan with ½ cup water; cover, bring to boil, remove from heat. By this time shells should have opened; if not, return to heat a few minutes more. Discard any mussel shells which do not open.

Fold shelled prawns and red and green pepper into rice. Cover and continue cooking for further 2 to 3 minutes to heat prawns and peppers.

Spoon paella on to serving dish, arrange mussels in shells decoratively round edge.

Serves 6.

Pineapple Chicken

1.5 kg (3 lb.) chicken pieces
½ cup flour
½ teaspoon ground ginger
1 tablespoon curry powder
salt, pepper
30 g (1 oz.) butter
1 tablespoon oil
1 clove garlic
450 g can crushed pineapple
1 cup water
1 chicken stock cube
3 sliced gherkins

Toss chicken in combined flour, ginger, curry powder, salt and pepper. Heat oil and butter in pan, add crushed garlic, sauté 1 minute; add chicken pieces, cook until golden brown, pour off surplus fat.

Add undrained pineapple and all remaining ingredients, cover, simmer 40 minutes, or until chicken is tender.

If desired, serve sprinkled with chopped mint.

Serves 4.

Pistachio Chicken

1.5 kg (3 lb.) chicken
1 onion
60 g (2 oz.) bacon
30 g (1 oz.) butter
250 g (8 oz.) sausage mince
3 cups fresh breadcrumbs
1 tablespoon chopped parsley
½ teaspoon mixed herbs
1 egg
185 g (6 oz.) pistachio nuts
salt, pepper

Melt butter in frying pan, add finely chopped onion and bacon, sauté until onion is transparent. Combine sausage mince, breadcrumbs, seasonings, onion and bacon mixture; mix with beaten egg. Add shelled pistachio nuts.

Bone chicken (see page 9).

Place stuffing into chicken, reshape, secure cut part at back of chicken with skewers. Bake in moderate oven 1½ hours or until chicken is tender. Serve hot or cold.

Serves 4.

Russian Kotlets

1.5 kg (3 lb.) chicken (or chicken pieces)
1 slice white bread
¼ cup milk
2 medium onions
2 eggs, separated
salt, pepper
packaged dry breadcrumbs
butter for frying
1 cup sour cream

Remove meat from chicken; discard bones and skin. Pour milk over bread in bowl. Put chicken meat, chopped onions, and soaked bread through mincer once. Place into mixing bowl. Add egg-yolks, salt and pepper and beat on electric mixer or mix well with hands until smooth. Fold in stiffly beaten egg-whites. Shape into small flat patties the size of an egg. Coat firmly with bread-crumbs, fry in hot butter until golden brown and cooked through. Transfer to serving dish. Add sour cream to pan juices and heat gently. Pour over kotlets.

Makes approximately 1½ dozen.

Sour-Cream Chicken

1 large onion
1.5 kg (3 lb.) chicken (or chicken pieces)
1 teaspoon salt
125 g (4 oz.) butter
1 tablespoon paprika
⅓ cup flour
1 cup water
1 chicken stock cube
1 cup sour cream
1 cup dry white wine
470 g can artichoke hearts
125 g (4 oz.) mushrooms

Chop onion finely; sprinkle chicken pieces with salt. Heat butter in frying pan, add chicken pieces, cook until golden brown; remove from pan, drain well. Add onion and paprika to pan, sauté until onion is soft. Remove pan from heat, stir in flour, return to heat, cook 1 minute. Gradually add water, then crumbled stock cube; stir until mixture boils and thickens. Add cream and wine, stir well, heat gently, do not boil.

Put chicken and sliced mushrooms in ovenproof dish, top with sauce, cover and bake in moderate oven 1 hour. Add artichoke hearts for last 10 minutes of cooking time.

If desired, garnish with 60 g (2 oz.) crisp fried crumbled bacon and 30 g (1 oz.) toasted slivered almonds before serving.

Serves 4.

Sherry Baked Chicken

4 slices green ginger
3 tablespoons dry sherry
2 tablespoons soy sauce
½ teaspoon curry powder
½ teaspoon sugar
1.5 kg (3 lb.) chicken pieces
60 g (2 oz.) butter

Peel and finely chop ginger, combine with sherry, soy sauce, curry powder, and sugar. Pour over chicken pieces, stand 2 hours, turning occasionally.

Put drained chicken pieces in baking dish, pour over melted butter. Bake in moderate oven 45 to 50 minutes, or until tender. Several times during cooking, brush chicken pieces with the remaining marinade.

Serves 4.

Whisky Chicken

4 whole chicken breasts
125 g (4 oz.) butter
¼ cup whisky
1 red pepper
1 cup cream
⅓ cup dry sherry
⅓ cup water
1 chicken stock cube
1 teaspoon lemon juice
salt, pepper

Carefully remove skin from chicken breasts, cut breasts in half, sauté in heated butter until brown, remove from pan. Add pepper, cut into thin strips, to pan drippings, sauté a few minutes, remove from pan. Add whisky to pan; when warmed, set aflame. Add cream, sherry, water, crumbled stock cube and lemon juice, blend well. Return chicken and pepper to pan, simmer slowly, covered, until chicken is tender. Season to taste with salt and pepper.

Serves 4.

Pistachio Chicken—boned chicken, filled with savoury seasoning and studded with colourful pistachio nuts— is equally good served hot, with vegetables, or cold with salad.

Soups

Full of flavour, these lovely soups make a perfect beginning to a meal; or, with sandwiches and salad, they're a light, yet satisfying luncheon or supper dish. And we've added some hearty soups that are substantial enough to be main-course meals in themselves.

Chicken Soup

3 chicken pieces
1 large onion
1 carrot
2 sticks celery
salt, pepper
6 cups water

Inexpensive chicken pieces, such as chicken backs, are excellent for soup. Put into saucepan, add finely chopped onion, chopped carrot and celery, salt and pepper and water. Bring to boil, skim well; reduce heat, simmer, covered, 1 hour.

Remove chicken pieces from pan, remove any chicken meat and return meat to saucepan. Add parsley. Two or three finely chopped shallots can be added with the parsley, and 1 teaspoon soy sauce can be stirred in to give a slightly darker colour to the soup.

Serves 4 to 6.

Note: The liquid in which a chicken has been boiled makes an excellent basis for chicken soup. After the chicken has cooked and been removed from the saucepan, skim the liquid well, return pan to heat and cook soup, rapidly, until liquid has been reduced by half; this concentrates the flavour. The soup can be strained, if desired, and chopped parsley and choppped shallots stirred in before serving.

Chicken and Rice Soup

4 cups chicken stock
pinch thyme
1 tablespoon rice
salt, pepper
250 g (8 oz.) vegetables (carrot, leek or onion, turnip, celery)
parsley

Bring chicken stock to the boil. Prepare vegetables, cut into 5 mm (¼ in.) dice. Add vegetables, thyme and rice to boiling stock; reduce heat, simmer until rice and vegetables are tender. Season with salt and pepper, sprinkle with chopped parsley.

Serves 4.

Farmhouse Chicken Soup

1 kg (2 lb.) chicken pieces
4 ripe tomatoes
1 small eggplant
1 large onion
4 cups water
60 g (2 oz.) butter
pinch oregano
salt, pepper
60 g (2 oz.) shell noodles or macaroni
boiling salted water

Peel and chop tomatoes, eggplant and onion. Melt butter in large saucepan, sauté onion until tender. Add chicken pieces, brown lightly all over. Add tomatoes, eggplant, water and seasonings. Bring to boil, reduce heat, simmer, covered, 1 hour, remove from heat, remove chicken pieces; cool.

Add noodles to boiling water, boil rapidly 10 minutes, or until tender; drain.

Remove meat from chicken bones, chop meat roughly. Add chicken meat and noodles to soup, season to taste; reheat gently.

Serves 4 as a main-meal soup.

Note: If eggplants are out of season, substitute 2 chopped sticks of celery and 1 or 2 chopped carrots.

Japanese Chicken Soup

4 cups fish stock
1 teaspoon soy sauce
½ teaspoon salt
4 mushrooms
1 chicken breast
1 tablespoon cornflour
1 tablespoon oil
½ lemon
2 shallots

Bring fish stock to boil, add soy sauce, salt and quartered mushrooms; reduce heat, cover, simmer 7 to 10 minutes.

Remove chicken meat from bones, cut into 2.5 cm (1 in.) pieces, coat lightly with cornflour. Heat oil in saucepan, fry chicken pieces until tender and pale golden brown; drain.

Wash and thinly peel ½ lemon, cut rind into very fine strips. Wash and chop shallots.

Put chicken pieces into base of each soup plate, pour in hot soup and mushroom pieces. Add a few strips of lemon and top with a few chopped shallots.

Serves 4.

Note: Some specialty shops which sell correct ingredients for Japanese cooking have packets of fish stock ideal for this soup; the packet stock contains powdered fish, prawns, seaweed, and is available in sachets of five packets, costing around 30 cents. One sachet is sufficient for 4 cups of fish stock. The Japanese soy sauce, lighter and slightly sweeter than the Chinese, is also available at these shops. In Sydney, these special Japanese ingredients are obtainable from Anegawa, 16a Deepwater Road, Castle Cove, 2069 and other Japanese food stores.

Curried Chicken Soup

15 g (½ oz.) butter
1 small onion
½ green pepper
2 teaspoons curry powder
440 g can chicken soup
1 cup water
1 cup sour cream
salt, pepper

Sauté chopped onion and green pepper in hot butter in pan until soft, add curry powder, cook few minutes. Add all remaining ingredients, stir over low heat until soup reaches boiling point, but do not allow to boil.

Serves 4.

Chicken Bisque

2 whole chicken breasts
60 g (2 oz.) butter
1 medium carrot
1 medium onion
1 cup dry white wine
4 cups water
1 chicken stock cube
45 g (1½ oz.) butter extra
2 tablespoons flour
½ cup cream
1 tablespoon brandy
salt, pepper

Melt 60 g (2 oz.) butter. Fry chicken lightly, do not brown. Remove from pan. Add finely chopped onion and carrot to pan. Replace chicken on top of vegetables, cover, cook very slowly until vegetables are tender, approximately 15 minutes. Add wine, simmer 10 minutes.

Lift out chicken, remove bones and skin, put meat through blender or chop finely and push through sieve.

Melt extra butter, stir in flour, cook few minutes. Remove from heat, gradually add water. Add crumbled stock cube. Return to heat, bring to boil, stirring. Add vegetables and chicken.

Season with salt and pepper. Just before serving, stir in cream and brandy, heat gently.

Serves 4 to 6.

Chicken-Macaroni Soup

1.5 kg (3 lb.) chicken
water
2 teaspoons salt
12 whole peppercorns
1 bayleaf
1 large onion
1 stick celery
1 clove garlic
1 medium carrot
90 g (3 oz.) butter
½ cup flour
440 g can whole tomatoes
2 tablespoons curry powder
2 tablespoons fruit chutney
salt, pepper
chopped parsley
⅓ cup shell macaroni
boiling salted water

Put chicken in large saucepan, cover with water. Add salt, peppercorns, and bayleaf. Bring to boil, reduce heat, simmer, covered, until tender. Drain; reserve 4 cups of the strained stock; cut chicken into cubes, discarding skin and bones.

Finely chop onion, celery and carrot; crush garlic. Sauté vegetables and garlic in butter in pan 5 minutes. Stir in flour and curry powder, cook few minutes. Remove from heat, gradually add reserved stock. Return to heat, stir until soup boils and thickens. Add chopped tomatoes with their liquid, chutney, salt and pepper. Bring to boil, reduce heat, simmer, covered, 45 minutes.

Cook macaroni in boiling salted water until tender, approximately 10 minutes, drain. Add chicken and macaroni to soup; reheat gently. Serve in deep bowls, sprinkle with parsley.

Serves 4 to 6 as a main-meal soup.

Chicken and Avocado Soup

440 g can chicken soup
milk
1 avocado
1 teaspoon lemon juice
1 tablespoon cream
salt, pepper

Choose a nice ripe avocado. Remove flesh from inside, push through fine sieve; mix in lemon juice immediately so that avocado keeps its fresh colour.

Put soup and a soup can full of milk into saucepan; bring to boiling point, stirring. Reduce heat, add avocado purée, cream, salt and pepper to taste. Heat very gently, do not boil.

Serves 4.

Note: This delicious soup takes only minutes to prepare. It is best prepared and heated just prior to serving; if over-cooked or over-heated, the avocado becomes bitter.

Cold Chicken Dishes

Salads or other cold dishes with chicken are excellent for summer-time meals. They're so attractive in presentation, they're ideal, too, for a smorgasbord or buffet party.

Curried Chicken Salad

1.5 kg (3 lb.) chicken, steamed
190 g can whole mushrooms
1 lettuce
1 cucumber
1 red pepper
300 g can asparagus cuts
½ cup french dressing
2 teaspoons curry powder

Remove bones and skin from chicken, cut meat into small serving-sized pieces. Drain mushrooms and asparagus. Wash lettuce, dry well. Cut peeled cucumber in half lengthwise; cut into slices. Cut pepper into thin strips.

Combine chicken pieces with all vegetables except lettuce.

Combine french dressing and curry powder, pour over salad, toss lightly. Arrange salad over lettuce in salad bowl.

Serves 4.

Chicken in Aspic

1.5 kg (3 lb.) chicken
1 carrot
1 stick celery
1 medium onion
1 clove garlic
1 bayleaf
piece of lemon rind
salt, pepper
1 tablespoon gelatine
3 tablespoons water
2 tablespoons chopped parsley

Place chicken in a pan with sliced carrot, sliced celery, sliced onion, crushed garlic, bayleaf, lemon rind and salt and pepper. Cover with water, bring to the boil; reduce heat, simmer until chicken is cooked.

Remove chicken from pan, remove meat from bone. Return bones and skin to pan and allow to boil a further 10 minutes. Cut meat into small pieces, chop parsley; sprinkle gelatine over the water.

Strain bones and vegetables from stock, then strain stock again through muslin to give a clear liquid.

Take 2 cups of hot stock and add the gelatine, add salt to taste. Mix together chicken, parsley and stock, pour into oiled mould. Refrigerate until set, stirring occasionally to distribute meat evenly.

Serves 4.

Chicken Chaud-Froid

2 whole chicken breasts
water
3 chicken stock cubes
1 bayleaf
6 whole peppercorns
1 onion
salt
30 g (1 oz.) butter
1½ tablespoons flour
½ cup cream
red and green peppers
stuffed olives
capers
parsley
1 tablespoon gelatine

Place chicken breasts in saucepan with just enough water to cover, add crumbled stock cubes, bayleaf, peppercorns, chopped onion, salt. Bring to boil, reduce heat, simmer, covered, 30 minutes. Strain, reserve stock.

Remove chicken breasts carefully from bones, cut in half, remove skin, trim meat to neat shape. Refrigerate until cold.

Melt butter in pan, stir in flour, cook 1 minute. Remove from heat, gradually add ½ cup of reserved stock. Return to heat, stir until sauce boils and thickens. Remove from heat, stir in cream, stir until smooth. Cool slightly, then spoon over chicken breasts to cover surface completely.

When sauce is set, decorate top attractively with various shapes cut from thinly sliced olives, thinly sliced green and red peppers, drained capers and tiny sprigs of parsley. Return to refrigerator until well chilled.

Sprinkle gelatine over 1 cup of reserved stock, leave until stock starts to set. Spoon gelatine mixture over chicken breasts, refrigerate until set.

Delicious as a first course; some small crisp lettuce leaves can be added to each serving.

Serves 4.

Chicken Salad in Aspic—surprisingly easy to make is this superb chicken dish. Cut into slices for an unusual entrée, or luncheon dish, or serve as one of the dishes for a buffet party. *See page 40.*

Chicken Salad in Aspic

1.5 kg (3 lb.) chicken pieces
1 onion
1 bayleaf
6 peppercorns
125 g (4 oz.) mushrooms
30 g (1 oz.) butter
4 shallots
1 cup mayonnaise
½ cup sour cream
500 g (1 lb.) packaged puff pastry
1 tablespoon gelatine
2 tablespoons water
2 tablespoons sour cream, extra
3 gherkins
salt, pepper

Place chicken in saucepan, add chopped onion, bay leaf and peppercorns; cover with water, cover, cook until chicken is tender. Remove chicken from saucepan, cool. Strain liquid and reserve 2 cups.

Sprinkle gelatine over water, add hot reserved chicken stock, stir until gelatine is dissolved; cool.

Roll out puff pastry to 30 cm (12 in.) square; cut in half. Place each half on to oven tray, bake in hot oven 5 to 8 minutes or until pastry is golden; cool.

Chop mushrooms finely, reserving a few small ones for decoration. Melt butter in saucepan, add mushrooms, sauté 2 to 3 minutes; cool.

Remove skin and bones from chicken; chop meat finely or put through mincer. Combine chicken meat, mushrooms, chopped shallots, mayonnaise, sour cream, salt and pepper; mix well.

Cut pastry to fit 20 cm x 10 cm (8 x 4 in.) loaf tin. Slice each piece of pastry through centre, horizontally. Beginning with pastry, layer pastry and chicken filling into loaf tin until all ingredients are used; finish with layer of pastry. Cover pastry at top with extra sour cream and arrange reserved sliced mushrooms and sliced gherkins decoratively on top.

When chicken stock just begins to set, pour carefully into loaf tin, making sure the aspic reaches the bottom of the tin.

Refrigerate overnight. Turn out carefully, reverse, so that decorated top is uppermost; cut into slices. Serve with salad.

Serves 6.

Chicken and Rice Salad

⅔ cup long-grain rice
1 cup diced cooked chicken
2 slices ham
¼ cup chopped celery
2 teaspoons chopped onion
⅓ cup mayonnaise
1 teaspoon curry powder
salt, pepper

Cook rice in large saucepan of boiling salted water for 12 minutes; drain, cool.

Combine chicken, diced ham, onion, celery and cooked rice. Blend curry powder, mayonnaise, salt and pepper, mix lightly through salad.

Refrigerate. Serve in crisp lettuce leaves.

Serves 2.

Avocado Chicken Salad

3 avocados
2 teaspoons lemon juice
1.5 kg (3 lb.) chicken, steamed
4 sticks celery
1 cucumber
½ cup cream
2 tablespoons mayonnaise
¼ cup toasted slivered almonds
½ green pepper
1 teaspoon paprika
½ teaspoon nutmeg
salt, pepper

Peel, seed and slice avocados. Remove chicken meat from bones. Cut meat into cubes. Line salad bowl with crisp lettuce leaves. Slice peeled cucumber, celery and green pepper; layer in bowl with toasted almonds, chicken and half the avocado slices.

Blend paprika, nutmeg, salt and pepper with cream, mayonnaise and lemon juice; pour over chicken and vegetables, toss lightly. Decorate with remaining avocado slices, sprinkle with extra paprika.

Note: If preparing this dish in advance, dip avocado slices in lemon juice so they will keep their fresh colour.

Serves 4 to 6.

Chicken with Grapes

1.5 kg (3 lb.) chicken, steamed or roasted
½ teaspoon dry mustard
salt, pepper
1 cup sour cream
½ cup mayonnaise
2 tablespoons dry white wine or dry sherry
6 shallots
454 g can white grapes
470 g can asparagus cuts
lettuce

Remove chicken meat from bones and cut into serving-sized pieces; discard skin.

In a bowl blend mustard, salt and pepper with a little sour cream. When smooth, add remaining sour cream, mayonnaise, and white wine; mix well.

Finely chop shallots, add to sour cream mixture with drained grapes (reserve a few for decorating finished salad) and drained asparagus. Add chicken pieces, mix lightly. Refrigerate ½ hour before serving.

Arrange salad on lettuce leaves, decorate with reserved grapes.

Serves 4.

Chicken Livers

Chicken livers can be transformed into delicious, easily-prepared entrées or main-course meals, or they can be the basis of superb pâtés.

Chicken Liver Pate

500 g (1 lb.) chicken livers
1 small onion
4 rashers bacon
30 g (1 oz.) butter
½ teaspoon salt
1 clove garlic
2 teaspoons brandy
2 tablespoons cream
pinch mixed herbs
2 hard-boiled eggs

Chop onion, dice bacon, cut cleaned livers in small pieces. Heat butter in saucepan, add onion and bacon, cover, cook gently 10 minutes or until tender. Add cleaned chicken livers, cook, stirring, until brown. Add salt, crushed garlic, brandy, cream, mixed herbs, and chopped eggs.

Put in blender and blend on high speed until smooth; push through sieve. Spoon into serving bowl and refrigerate. Serve with hot toast.

Pate with Port

250 g (8 oz.) chicken livers
30 g (1 oz.) butter
1 small onion
¼ teaspoon thyme
1 small bayleaf
3 rashers bacon
1 tablespoon port
1 tablespoon dry sherry
salt, pepper
⅓ cup cream
1 teaspoon brandy
60 g (2 oz.) mushrooms

Clean and dry chicken livers. Heat butter in pan, sauté livers, finely chopped onion, thyme, bayleaf, chopped mushrooms, and chopped bacon 7 to 10 minutes. Remove from heat, discard bayleaf.

Put mixture in blender with cream, blend until smooth; push through sieve. Stir in port, sherry, and brandy. Season with salt and pepper. Refrigerate until cold.

Serve with hot toast.

Chicken Livers with Madeira

500 g (1 lb.) chicken livers
30 g (1 oz.) butter
1 small onion
1 rasher bacon
60 g (2 oz.) mushrooms
2 tablespoons chopped parsley

Madeira Sauce:

45 g (1½ oz.) butter
2 tablespoons flour
1 chicken stock cube
¾ cup water
½ cup madeira
salt, pepper

Soak cleaned chicken livers in warm water 10 minutes. Dry well, cut into 4. Heat butter, sauté chopped onion, chopped bacon, and sliced mushrooms. Add chicken livers, cook gently 10 to 15 minutes.

Stir in Madeira Sauce, heat through gently, stir in chopped parsley. Serve with hot rice.

Sauce: Melt butter, remove from heat, blend in flour. Return to heat and cook for 2 minutes, stirring. Remove from heat, gradually add water then crumbled stock cube; stir until smooth. Return to heat, stir until sauce boils and thickens. Add madeira, season with salt and pepper.

Serves 4.

Chicken Liver Risotto

500 g (1 lb.) chicken livers
2 onions
125 g (4 oz.) butter
2 cups long grain rice
3 sticks celery
4½ cups chicken stock
salt, pepper
½ cup grated parmesan cheese

Heat half the butter in large saucepan. Add finely chopped onions and sliced celery, sauté 10 minutes, stirring occasionaly.

Cut cleaned chicken livers into quarters. Add to pan, cook further 5 minutes. Stir in well-washed rice and remaining butter, cook further 5 minutes. Add stock, bring to the boil; reduce heat and simmer, covered, until rice is tender and liquid absorbed, 20 to 25 minutes. Stir in parmesan cheese. Season with salt and pepper.

Serves 6.

Recipes from Restaurants

A particular chicken dish is a specialty on the menus of many of Australia's most popular restaurants. Our thanks go to the restaurants featured here, who have been happy to share with our readers their delicious creations.

Breast of Chicken Beppi

(Beppi's, Sydney)

2 whole chicken breasts
salt, pepper
flour
4 tablespoons oil
30 g (1 oz.) butter
1 clove garlic
6 capers
2 teaspoons chopped parsley
4 slices mozzarella cheese
4 anchovy fillets
½ cup marsala
¼ cup cream

Halve chicken breasts lengthwise. Season with salt and pepper, roll lightly in flour. Cook in hot oil until golden brown and tender, about 10 minutes, turning occasionally. Drain off oil, add butter to pan with chicken. Add crushed garlic, chopped capers and parsley. Top each chicken breast with a slice of cheese and sliced anchovy fillet. Pour marsala over chicken, simmer gently 3 minutes. Place chicken on serving dishes. Add cream to pan, stir well. Pour sauce over chicken.

Serves 4.

Poulet a la Corse

(La Causerie, Kings Cross, Sydney)

1.5 kg (3 lb.) chicken
250 g (8 oz.) bacon rashes
250 g (8 oz.) small mushrooms
125 g (4 oz.) black olives
500 g (1 lb.) tomatoes
2 cloves garlic
salt, pepper
½ teaspoon basil
500 g (1 lb.) small potatoes
½ cup brandy
½ cup chicken stock
chopped parsley

Chop bacon finely, sauté until crisp; remove from pan; cook chicken in this bacon fat until well browned; add a little butter to pan, if necessary. Put chicken, with pan juices, into casserole.

Add sliced mushrooms, bacon pieces, crushed garlic, basil, salt and pepper to chicken; cover casserole, bake in moderately hot oven 30 minutes.

Wash olives, add to casserole with peeled, sliced potatoes and peeled, chopped tomatoes. Reduce oven heat to moderate; cook chicken uncovered, further 30 minutes, or until chicken and potatoes are tender.

Warm brandy, pour over chicken, set aflame; let flames die out.

Cut chicken into serving pieces, surround with the mushrooms and potatoes. Add hot chicken stock to casserole, stir well, pour over chicken; sprinkle with chopped parsley.

Serve with a green salad.

Serves 4.

Breast of Chicken with Hazelnut-Cream Sauce

(Fanny's, Melbourne)

2 whole chicken breasts
salt, pepper
flour
60 g (2 oz.) butter
1 tablespoon oil
¾ cup port wine
1 cup cream
¾ cup chopped hazelnuts

Bone chicken breasts, cut in halves; flatten with mallet. Season to taste with salt and pepper, roll in flour. Heat oil and butter in pan, sauté chicken breasts 5 minutes on each side. Pour off excess fat from pan. Add wine to pan, cook 2 minutes, or until wine is reduced by half. Add cream and cook further 2 minutes until reduced by half again. Add hazelnuts, cook further 2 minutes.

Accompaniments at the restaurant are whole french beans and Pommes Soufflé.

Serves 4.

Chinese Curried Chicken

(The Mandarin, Sydney)

1 kg (2 lb.) chicken
2 medium potatoes
30 g (1 oz.) dried mushrooms
6 shallots
2 large onions
oil for deep frying
2 tablespoons oil, extra
2 tablespoons curry powder
salt
¾ cup evaporated milk
2 cups chicken stock
3 tablespoons cornflour
½ teaspoon sesame oil

Chicken-Pineapple casserole—the good, fresh taste of pineapple teams deliciously with chicken and bacon in this easy-to-make casserole. See page 25.

Have chicken at room temperature. Drop chicken into large boiler of boiling water, cover with firm fitting lid, bring back to boil, turn off heat, leave covered and allow to stand overnight. Remove chicken from water, wash under cold running water until chicken is completely cold. Remove bones and skin from chicken, cut meat into 5 cm x 5 mm (2 in. x ¼ in.) strips.

Peel potatoes, cut into 2 cm (¾ in.) dice, deep fry in hot oil until golden brown, drain. Cover dried mushrooms with hot water, stand 20 minutes. Cut into fine strips, about 5 mm (¼ in.) wide. Chop shallots into 2.5 cm (1 in.) pieces. Peel onions, slice into long strips.

Heat extra oil in large heavy-based frying pan, add mushrooms, shallots, onions and curry powder, sauté until onion is just tender. Add chicken, potatoes and milk, season to taste with salt, cook until well heated.

Blend cornflour with stock, add to pan with sesame oil, stir constantly until mixture boils and thickens.

Serves 4.

Chicken Sultana

(Maxim's, Melbourne)

(At the request of Sir William Oliver, who was then British High Commissioner in Australia, this recipe was supplied to his chef in Canberra and served at a luncheon in honour of Queen Elizabeth when she visited Australia with the Duke of Edinburgh. For this royal occasion, the dish was re-named Chicken Maxim's).

2 whole chicken breasts
3 rashers bacon
2 tablespoons chopped almonds
olive oil
60 g (2 oz.) butter
flour
salt, pepper

Bone chicken breasts, cut in halves to get 4 pieces; flatten with mallet. Season to taste wiith salt and pepper. Coat lightly with flour. Brush all over with oil. Place under hot griller 5 minutes each side, turning occasionally.

Combine chopped bacon and almonds and place on top of chicken breasts. Dot with butter. Place in baking dish, bake in hot oven 7 minutes, until golden brown. Remove and place again under griller until bacon is crisp, approximately 2 minutes. Serve with hot vegetables or tossed salad.

Serves 4.

'Billy Kee' Chicken

(Taiping, Sydney)

1.5 kg (3 lb.) chicken
3 egg-yolks
oil for deep frying
½ cup tomato sauce
½ cup dry red wine
1 teaspoon worcestershire sauce
salt

Remove meat from uncooked chicken, discarding skin. Chop chicken into 4 cm (1½ in.) pieces, add to beaten egg-yolks; mix well.

Deep-fry chicken in hot oil until lightly browned, drain well.

Combine wine and sauces in large heavy-based frying pan. When hot, add chicken pieces, heat and mix well; season to taste with salt. Garnish with pineapple pieces.

Serves 3.

Chicken Saute Castillane

(Wentworth Hotel, Sydney)

1.5 kg (3 lb.) chicken
6 shallots
flour
½ teaspoon oregano
salt, pepper
⅓ cup oil
1 tablespoon brandy
1 clove garlic
⅓ cup dry white wine
2 tablespoon cream
½ teaspoon thinly sliced orange rind
chopped parsley

Joint and bone chicken; cut breasts in half and legs in half. Season a little flour with salt, pepper and oregano. Roll chicken pieces in seasoned flour.

Heat oil in large pan until piping hot, add chicken and cook over high heat until golden brown on both sides; pour off excess oil from pan.

Keeping pan over heat, pour brandy over chicken, ignite and wait for brandy to burn out completely. Add shallots, cut into 2.5 cm (1 in.) lengths, and finely chopped garlic, cook slowly a few minutes. Pour in wine and bring quickly to boil, add cream and orange rind, reduce heat to low. Cover, simmer gently 10 to 15 minutes. Sprinkle with chopped parsley; serve with boiled potatoes or rice.

Serves 4.

Index